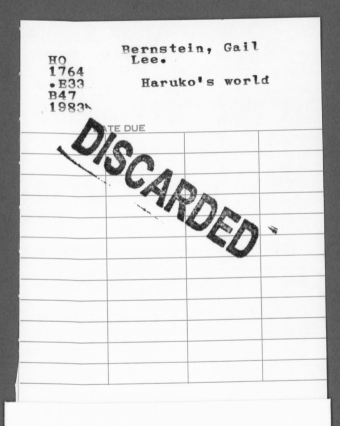

Haruko's World

HARUKO'S WORLD

*A Japanese Farm Woman and
Her Community*

GAIL LEE BERNSTEIN

Stanford University Press, Stanford, California

1983

Stanford University Press
Stanford, California
© 1983 by the Board of Trustees of the
Leland Stanford Junior University
Printed in the United States of America
ISBN 0–8047–1174–7
LC 82–61783

Dedicated to the memory of
Robert Hurley (1926–1969) and
to Judith W. Hurley, who
planted the seeds for this study
and for so much else

Acknowledgments

AMONG THE MANY PEOPLE who contributed to this book, I should like to give special thanks to the following students, colleagues, mentors, and friends. Jean and Hiroki Shioji made it all possible by arranging for my homestay with the Utsunomiya family. Ezra Vogel offered practical advice at the outset. Takeshi Ishida, who has always been indispensable in facilitating my research, this time made an on-site inspection to help confirm my own research findings and impressions. Carl Tomizuka spent many hours talking over the material with me. Tomone Matsumoto helped translate Haruko Utsunomiya's thirty-six-page handwritten autobiography, and Shizuko Radbill lent her considerable skills as a reference librarian. J. G. Bell, Pamela Gilbreath, J. Michael Mahar, Thomas A. Stanley, Jayne Werner, and Margery Wolf read the manuscript at various stages and offered editorial advice and sorely needed encouragement. Louise Fields, flawless typist and perceptive reader, provided me with the built-in audience I needed to focus the contents of the book. Hiroshi Wagatsuma read the penultimate draft, and with his keen ear for language improved both the translation of Japanese terms and the text as a whole. Stanford University Press's thoughtful and conscientious outside reviewer saved me from some embarrassing slips of the pen, and Production Editor John Feneron labored over the final draft with tact and patience.

My research for the book was generously supported by a grant from the Japan Foundation in 1974–75. A grant from the University of Arizona Foundation helped defray typing costs. I am grateful to both foundations.

Three people were involved in this book whose generosity I can never sufficiently repay. Michael Patrick Sullivan, an indefatigable supporter of the project from its inception, kept me on course with his unbounded enthusiasm, his editorial suggestions, and his wise counsel. Haruko and Shō-ichi Utsunomiya shared their lives with me, and are not only the subjects but the silent co-authors of the book.

G.L.B.

Contents

Introcuction

💠

THIS IS A PORTRAIT of contemporary rural Japanese women viewed primarily through the eyes of one woman, Haruko Utsunomiya, with whose family I lived in Ehime prefecture from October 1974 to May 1975. My presentation is a personal one: in addition to describing the women, their work, and their family life, I hope to capture something of their feelings, problems, and aspirations—topics that are often neglected in conventional village studies. By the same token, many of the topics traditionally examined by ethnographers are absent here.

Throughout Japan's history, women have played an important role in agriculture. Today only about six million persons are actively engaged in farming in Japan—about five percent of the population—but not too long ago the proportion was eighty percent. Women's labor was crucial to the cultivation of the main crop, rice, and of cash crops and vegetables for the family table. In the past 150 years, women have also contributed significantly to the farm family's income by earning wages as textile workers, day laborers, or household servants. And within the past two decades, as a result of the exodus of male workers to the cities, women have emerged as the mainstay of Japanese agriculture: over one-half of Japan's farmers are female.

To observe the lives of farm women today is to recapture something of Japan's past, but it is also to record the great changes overtaking rural Japan. Even while I was living with Haruko's family, momentous events were occurring in their lives. The introduction of farm machinery—pioneered in their hamlet by Haruko's husband

—promised to alter the nature of women's traditional work. Haruko and her family, like farm families throughout Japan, stand at a crossroads: the mechanization of agriculture is revolutionizing the face of the countryside and with it the fabric of family life. Because Haruko was aware of the importance of these changes and because, as a representative of a transitional generation, she could look both backward and forward in time, her life story is an especially valuable historical chronicle.

Although my research in Ehime focused on Haruko, it also extended to other farm women in the four townships that make up Higashiuwa county: Uwa, Shirokawa, Nomura, and Akehama. Uwa, the bustling hub of the county, was my home base. Shirokawa and Nomura are remote mountainous areas whose farmers barely manage to coax a crop from the soil. The last township, Akehama, is a fishing community pressed between mountains and the sea. I chose this area of Japan because one of my Japanese graduate students knew Haruko's husband and offered to arrange my home stay with the family. Indeed, it would have been impossible for a foreigner to gain entry into a farming community without such personal connections.

Initially, an important consideration for me was the climate. As I had discovered on previous research trips to Tokyo and Kyoto, it can be difficult to live without central heating in Japan's damp, cold winters. But Ehime prefecture, noted for its mild winter climate, seemed ideal. Located on Shikoku, the smallest of Japan's four main islands, this southwestern prefecture is warm enough to sustain a thriving citriculture industry, and the rolling green mountains that run from north to south across its length are dotted with *mikan* (Japanese tangerine) orchards. What I did not learn until I arrived, however, was that Uwa township, home of my host family, was markedly colder, receiving more snow than any other part of Shikoku. The township, situated about seven miles from the coast in the central portion of Ehime, is in fact too cold for citrus fruit, and its major crop is rice. "We're at a higher altitude than the rest of the region," my host explained, almost apologetically, when the first blizzard came in De-

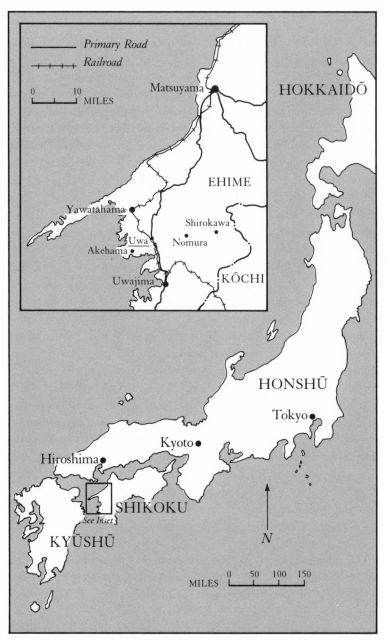

Map of Japan, showing Ehime prefecture (inset).

cember. By then, the family was humorously referring to my room as the icebox, and I wrote my nightly journal entries wearing mittens.

Uwa has been an important center of commerce and political life since the sixteenth century, and it is the second largest township in the prefecture. Located in a broad basin, it had a population in 1974 of 18,000 people, divided among fifty hamlets. All of Uwa is served by the governmental and trade facilities of the town of Unomachi, which is the site of the main branch of the Uwa Agricultural Co-operative, the Uwa Town Hall, and the central post office for the region. Unomachi is also a major express stop on the national railway line that connects the southern part of the prefecture with Matsu-yama, the prefectural capital to the northeast. In or near Unomachi are Akeishi Buddhist temple, famous as one of the eighty-eight stops on a popular pilgrimage through Shikoku, the ruins of a castle that was once the residence of a feudal lord, a bank, and Uwa's junior and senior high schools. Even on first impression the town presented an air of prosperity and vigor.

One mile west of Unomachi lived Haruko and her family, in the hamlet of Bessho. When I first met Haruko, her world was confined to the few miles that separate Bessho from Unomachi and from her parents' hamlet on the other side of Unomachi. Once or twice a week she rode her motor scooter down the one-lane paved road to town, usually to buy one or two specific items of food or clothing, and more rarely to visit one of the public offices or religious sites. Occasionally, when she wanted to buy a special gift or visit a friend in the hospital, she took the train south to the city of Uwajima, thirty minutes away. Once or twice a year she rode a chartered bus north to Yawatahama, another large city, to attend the annual meeting of the Ehime Women's Guild. On New Year's Day, her husband drove her to her parents' hamlet, two miles away.

Haruko had been out of the prefecture only three times in her life. In junior high school, she went on a school excursion to Kyoto, the ancient capital of Japan. On her honeymoon in 1956, she spent three days in Kyūshū, the island west of Shikoku, and in 1971 she spent an entire week with her husband in Tokyo—the high point of her life. Her dream is still to take a vacation in Hokkaidō, the northernmost island of Japan. Perhaps in another ten years, when her two children are married and she and her husband are no longer farming, she can realize that dream.

For most of her life, however, Haruko's world was limited to the hamlet in which she grew up and the hamlet of Bessho, to which she went when she was married, and her days were spent either in the rice paddies and vegetable fields or in the house of her husband's parents. She was forty-two years old when I first met her in 1974, and although she repeatedly insisted that she was a "typical Japanese farm woman," her outgoing personality and her willingness to share her innermost thoughts with me made her unique among the women of her community.

I have chosen an unconventional way to narrate Haruko's story. In the belief that my relations with her and with the other people I met in rural Japan form an important dimension of my account, I have allowed myself to appear in the pages of this book. Although this subjective approach has a number of academic precedents,* the reasons for my adopting it require some explanation.

First, Haruko's relationship with me revealed aspects of her personality that seemed impossible to ignore without doing damage to the very thing I most wanted to capture: the lives of real persons. Second, the reaction of rural Japanese in general to foreigners in their midst was a datum virtually absent in other village studies, not only because professional anthropologists are properly taught not to intrude their own feelings, but also because no anthropologist of Japan who has lived within a Japanese farm household for an extended period has written about that particular experience.† Finally, it was in the relations between myself and my Japanese hosts—and particu-

---

*Among the many researchers who speak in their own character in their published accounts of their fieldwork are Paul Rabinow, *Reflections on Fieldwork in Morocco* (Berkeley, Calif., 1977), and Jean Briggs, *Never in Anger: Portrait of an Eskimo Family* (Cambridge, Mass., 1970).

†This is not to say that previous scholars of Japan have neglected the human dimensions of Japanese life; see, for example, Ronald P. Dore, *Shinohata* (New York, 1978), and Robert J. Smith, *Kurusu* (Stanford, Calif., 1978). Also, Elly Lury Wiswell, widow of the pioneer anthropologist John Embree, kept a private journal of her life in village Japan in the 1930's, which she and Robert J. Smith have edited for publication as *The Women of Suye Mura* (Chicago, 1982).

larly in areas where our relations became most strained—that the clearest examples of cultural difference resided. But if these tensions were painful, I hope they may also prove instructive to others less familiar with Japanese society; and if my description of them is frank, it should not be taken as mocking anyone but myself.

In writing this study, I drew upon a variety of sources: my own observations of everyday family life, my interviews with farm women and Women's Guild leaders in Higashiuwa county, the answers to a written questionnaire I distributed to thirty women in the county, and published materials on farm women, such as government surveys and magazines put out by the Women's Guild. Also, at my request, Haruko set down her own life story on thirty-six handwritten pages. Long discussions with her and with her husband supplemented the other sources.

Part I of the book introduces Haruko, her family, and her environment. It also presents the methodological and personal problems involved in a foreign, female scholar's entry into the Japanese farm community. Part II begins with Haruko's life story, based largely on her autobiographical account. Readers are cautioned that Haruko's views of her husband and of her circumstances may differ from my own portrait of her elsewhere in the book; the value of a researcher's direct observation is precisely that it offers a different perspective from the one gained in formal interviews, life histories, or autobiographical accounts. Part II continues with descriptions of the mechanization program introduced by Haruko's husband, of Haruko's work, and of family interactions. The vignettes of the farm community in Part III center on social life, but also include a portrait of a farm woman quite different from Haruko, one whose personality therefore offers a sharp contrast with that of the book's central subject. The Epilogue, which is based on my return visit to Haruko's family in 1982, summarizes the major changes in her life and the lives of other farm women in the seven years since my initial fieldwork.

In anthropological writings of this sort it is conventional to change the names of persons and places in order to protect their privacy. I toyed with the idea of following this convention but in the end decided to yield to the wishes of Haruko and Shō-ichi, who very much wanted the book to be a documentary account of their lives. Where it was not practically possible to gain the consent of others or where I felt that for various reasons the use of real names was undesirable, I have used fictitious names.

PART I
Scholar and Subject

I
Arrival

HARUKO'S HUSBAND WAS standing in the waiting room of the railroad station when I got off the train at Unomachi. He was wearing a gray, long-sleeved shirt, baggy gray trousers, boots, and a cap, and he smelled faintly of pigs. Short and stocky, Mr. Utsunomiya had a full, round face and skin that was almost chocolate brown. Having spoken to him once on the telephone from Tokyo, I already knew that he had a soft, gentle voice. Later I learned that he was forty-five years old and that his given name was Shō-ichi.

We stumbled over introductions, both of us mumbling inaudibly, and immediately he led the way to a small white pick-up truck. The main street through the town was a lively avenue lined with specialty shops selling cakes, children's toys, underwear, stationery, tobacco, and the like. A red-and-white Coca Cola sign hung over a fruit store. Children in navy blue uniforms rode bicycles home from school, weaving in and out among cars, motor bikes, and an occasional large white bus. This city scene, complete with traffic lights, dirty gray public buildings, two supermarkets, and a coffee shop with its incongruous name Pony written in English, was anything but the rustic village setting I had expected.

In less than five minutes, however, we had left the town of Unomachi behind us. Crossing a single railroad track and then a small bridge over the Uwa River, we entered the countryside, heading west along a narrow, one-lane, paved road that wound around the edge of green rice paddies. It was late October, and the harvest was almost over. Yellow stalks of rice hung drying on wooden poles. Across the wide expanse of paddy fields to the north were clusters of houses, each representing a separate hamlet of thirty or forty households. The paddies were set in a valley of over 280 acres, encircled by low, green mountains. Irrigation ponds, one for each of the six hamlets surrounding the paddies, dotted the landscape and glistened in the sun. Lining both sides of the road we traveled were more houses—unpainted, single-story, windowless structures, some looking almost like shacks. Other houses were scattered along paths leading off from the paved road. Together these dwellings, spread along one mile of the road, constituted my ultimate destination, the hamlet of Bessho.

Although the characters used to write Bessho mean "special place" or "separate place," the close grouping of houses, storage sheds, and gardens conformed to no apparent order that might have given the hamlet a distinctive identity or a focal point. In Bessho, as in other hamlets in the area, most of the houses stood so close to one or two others that their roofs almost touched one another, and no pattern was discernible save that most of the houses faced south to take advantage of the winter sun. The houses were not numbered, though they were organized, at least in residents' minds, into three *kumi*, or groupings, roughly conforming to the eastern, central, and western portions of Bessho. Some families had hung a wooden plaque bearing their surname over their front door, but others had made no such effort to identify their residence. Shō-ichi could not even say with certainty how many families lived in Bessho, because young couples, after living for a few years with the husband's parents, often moved to smaller dwellings attached to the main house or a few yards away from it, and at least in official Post Office records, these did not count as separate households.

Every available inch of space around each house was put to good use. The space behind a house or between it and the shed resembled not so much a yard as a junk shop, for it was used to store old pots and pans, piles of long logs, or paper trash that was bagged in rice sacks and later burned. Most families had planted rows of vegetables in the few feet of dirt in front of their house. Several families also kept two or three hens in outdoor cages; others kept a single goat or cow tethered in a barn; and two families had dogs as pets, but these too were tied up outside the house.

We passed few people on our five-minute drive from town: the hamlet was oddly still. The casual observer might have concluded from the apparent absence of inhabitants that Bessho had recently been abandoned, but in fact it has approximately two hundred people, in about forty-five households. The hamlet was recorded as an administrative unit of government in 1588, and Shō-ichi's ancestors had lived there in the Tokugawa period (1600–1868).

Before I could ask Shō-ichi about the hamlet's residents, he slowed the truck as we approached one of the more spacious-looking dwellings, a house squeezed between the road and the paddies. Turning onto a dirt path alongside a goldfish pond, he shut off the engine, got out, and walked toward the house. The heavy wood door was closed but not locked; sliding it open, he entered the house ahead of me, carrying my two suitcases.

I followed Shō-ichi into the entryway, removed my shoes, and stepped up into the *chanoma*, or "tea room," a nine-foot-square windowless room with sliding doors instead of walls on three sides. The room, which served as the parlor or living room, was raised above the ground, lined with tatami (thickly padded mats made of straw and rush), and furnished with four floor cushions, a telephone, and an enormous color console-television set. In the center of the room was a low formica-top table, which straddled the *kotatsu*.* Shō-ichi invited me to sit down and grunted something in the direction of the kitchen.

Immediately his wife, Haruko, appeared beyond an open sliding door. She was standing a foot below us on the stone ground of the corridor that ran along one side of the house from the entryway in the front to the kitchen in the back. Before I could even rattle off appropriate words of greeting, she began apologizing or, rather, explaining why it was clearly impossible for me to stay with her family as we had arranged.

*The *kotatsu* is essentially a hole in the floor in which heated coals are placed. A heavy quilt is drawn over the table that straddles the hole, and families sit under the quilt, with their feet near the coals.

Though I barely understood her dialect, I gathered that she was worried about what to feed me and afraid we would be unable to communicate with one another. Punctuating her words with a raucous laugh, she added that all the villagers would stare at me because they were not accustomed to foreigners.

Haruko's husband interrupted this nervous recital by telling her to bring out some tea. Ignoring him, she continued with her list of all the reasons she could not possibly put me up: the house was too small, the only available room was probably inadequate for my needs, and her family were only poor farmers who did not eat the large portions of meat I was probably used to. What, after all, she wanted to know, was my purpose in coming to Bessho?

Accustomed as I was to the exquisite tact and good manners of urban Japanese friends, who immediately brought out hot towels, green tea, and fruit to refresh their guests and scrupulously avoided any question more taxing than whether the guests preferred to bathe before or after dinner, I was completely unprepared for my hostess's forthrightness. Having traveled since early morning by taxi, ferry, bus, and train from Hiroshima, for six hours by train from Tokyo the day before, and for fourteen hours by plane from the United States two days before that, I had been looking forward to some traditional Japanese pampering. Instead, I seemed to be in the way.

I explained that I had been a student of Japan for fifteen years and had lived before with Japanese families, so I would not have any difficulty understanding the language provided everybody spoke slowly. With each second, however, I was losing confidence in my ability ever to understand her or her husband, whose dialect sounded only remotely like the standard Japanese I had learned. I assured her with more conviction than I actually felt that I could eat everything and anything she cared to prepare. Finally, I explained that my purpose in boarding with her family was to study the everyday life of farm women. I was deliberately vague about my ultimate goals, however; as a "participant-observer," I was there, after all, to snoop.

To my dismay, my simply stated answers did not seem to satisfy her, but her husband indicated, by pointing his right elbow in the direction of the kitchen, that she should quickly bring the tea and not ask so many questions. After tea, my host and hostess fell silent. Trying hard to swallow my sense of discomfort, I asked to be shown my room and suggested that perhaps their teenage daughter, a junior high school student, might give me a tour of the hamlet. My hope was that she could speak standard Japanese and a few words of English, enough to help me through the first days of adjustment.

Shō-ichi led me to the room assigned to me, then left to summon his daughter. My room, which was lined with eight tatami, was the largest one in the house and was ordinarily used only on formal occasions to entertain guests. At one end was the *tokonoma*, a raised alcove six feet wide and about a foot deep, in which a scroll painting hung. On the floor of the alcove, below the painting, on a black lacquer base was a large bowl that should have contained a fresh floral decoration but instead stood empty, except for stale water and a metal clasp that once held flowers. In the corner of the alcove stood an arrow—a good-luck token from a nearby Shintō shrine where Shō-ichi's ancestors had served as priests—and two framed documents, which proved to be official letters of thanks to Shō-ichi for his service as head of the local Parent-Teacher Association and as a member of the town assembly. The only other decoration in the room was a large framed photograph of Shō-ichi's father, hanging in the space between the ceiling and the top of the paper sliding door that separated my room from the smaller one in which Shō-ichi and his wife slept. In every other farm house I visited, I would find similarly sober, unsmiling patriarchs, dressed in black robes and peering down on guests from their perches below the ceiling.

The room had no window and only one overhead light fixture. The west wall consisted of built-in closets stuffed with old newspapers, clothes, a vacuum cleaner, cartons—only Haruko knew precisely what was in there and where. In one corner of the room stood a narrow bookcase filled with the works of well-known modern Japanese novelists and also books on agriculture. (Shō-ichi had completed a college degree in horticulture in a correspondence course from a college outside Tokyo.) On the floor was a low, formica-top

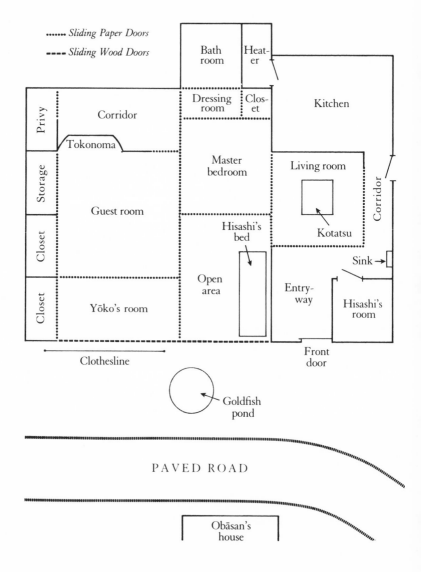

RICE PADDIES

N

...... *Sliding Paper Doors*
---- *Sliding Wood Doors*

Bath room

Heat-er

Privy

Corridor

Dressing room

Clos-et

Kitchen

Tokonoma

Master bedroom

Living room

Storage

Guest room

Kotatsu

Corridor

Closet

Hisashi's bed

Open area

Sink →

Closet

Yōko's room

Entry-way

Hisashi's room

Clothesline

Front door

Goldfish pond

PAVED ROAD

Obāsan's house

The Utsunomiyas' house.

table, a floor cushion, and a pile of bedding, including two mattresses and two heavy quilts that would serve as my bed, and a small, hard pillow that felt like a bean bag. Five of the twelve cartons of books and clothing I had mailed from the United States were piled in another corner.

A faint fecal odor emanated from somewhere just behind the *tokonoma*, and a brief search along the wood-floored corridor to the north of my room uncovered the location of the Japanese-style privy —a small room containing only a porcelain urinal and next to it a hole in the floor that the user squats over. I soon came to appreciate this indoor outhouse for its view, because, with the exception of the corridor, it was the only room in the house that had transparent glass windows, which looked out on the rice paddies that ran to the very base of the house.

The narrow corridor outside the privy was crowded with furniture, since it served as a kind of storage area or adjunct bedroom for Haruko, and contained her sewing machine, a legless vanity table that rested directly on the floor and supported both a full-size mirror and a floor-to-ceiling chest of drawers, or *tansu*, where Haruko stored her kimono and kimono accessories. The mirror and the *tansu* are standard items in the Japanese bride's dowry, as are the bedding and the shoe closet that stands in the entryway of Japanese houses. Another high chest, this one squeezed up against part of the sliding door to the privy, held a pile of coarse toilet-paper squares.

At the opposite end of the corridor from the privy was a paper-covered sliding door leading to a small dressing room, where family members removed their clothes before sliding open another door leading to the sunken bath room. The bath room was just that—a room used only for bathing. It housed a deep, square tub, lined with pale blue tile, and one other modern acquisition: a washing machine. A gas heater in a small room beyond the bath room supplied hot water. The bath had been installed six years earlier to accommodate a young American 4-H Club member who had stayed with the family for two weeks as part of a summertime exchange program; before that, the family had used the communal bathhouse still shared by several other families in the hamlet. Learning that once again an American woman would be living in the house, neighbors had asked my host whether he planned to introduce further innovations, such as a western-style toilet.

Shō-ichi returned with his daughter, Yōko, who was assigned to show me the rest of the house and did so in a noncommittal, diffident manner. A hearty-looking fifteen-year-old, Yōko had a round face, and a short, pixie-style, scalloped haircut. She took me first to see her room, adjacent to mine on the south side of the house. To reach it from the bath room, we walked back through my room. Because there was no hallway down the center of the house, or along the west wall, the most direct route to and from the bath room or the privy was either through my room or through the smaller room east of mine occupied by Haruko and Shō-ichi.

Yōko's room resembled an indoor veranda, its entire south wall a set of sliding wooden doors that opened onto the front garden. Nevertheless, a remarkable assortment of items were crammed into this narrow, twelve-foot by six-foot area: a bed, given to Yōko by relatives, a chest of drawers, a cardboard closet, a doll collection in a glass box, a desk, a chair, and a small organ. Yōko told me that she and her twelve-year-old brother, Hisashi, had slept with their parents until three years earlier, when both were given their own sleeping quarters.

Hisashi slept on a bed in a curtained-off corner of the open area just outside Yōko's room. The rest of this area served as a walkway from Yōko's room, her parents' room, and mine to the living room, and also as a repository for the laundry taken from the clothesline. The line—actually a blue plastic pole—was hung just beyond the sliding wood doors, which, when open, exposed most of the south side of the house, including Yōko's room and Hisashi's sleeping area, not only to the light of day and the goldfish pond, but also to the beep of car horns and the eyes of passing neighbors.

Our house tour was abruptly interrupted by Haruko, calling to us from the kitchen that dinner was ready. Getting to the kitchen, which was adjacent to the bath room and set on a stone floor on the same level as the east corridor, required some more logistical maneuvering.

We crossed through the living room, removed our house slippers, put on a pair of heeled shoes used for walking on the ground, and stepped down into the east corridor, which connected the kitchen in the rear with the entryway in the front. A dirty white enamel sink standing in the corner of this corridor was the family's washbasin, the equivalent of the bathroom sink in a western home. After using the toilet, family members had to trek from the northwest corner of the house to the southeast corner, change shoes, and step down into this chilly corridor in order to wash their hands. Soggy toothbrushes, a tiny round mirror, and damp hand towels hung on the wall over the sink, and an overhead aluminum rack held more towels, headgear, gloves, a large box of soapflakes, a red plastic glass—all further evidence of the cramped quarters and inadequate space in this drafty and dark house.

Peering around the corner, I noticed a room just off the entryway that was allocated to the Utsunomiyas' son, whose desk and guitar, along with a carton of tangerines, filled the entire space. Hisashi greeted me with a polite hello. Aside from an occasional "thank you" and "telephone call," the shy, thin twelve-year-old said little else to me for the remainder of my stay in Bessho.

In the kitchen, the family, crowded around a wrought-iron table, was joined by Shō-ichi's sixty-six-year-old mother, who lived in a two-room house across the road. We were given the briefest of introductions by Shō-ichi, who said simply, "This is my mother," as the tiny woman took her place opposite me. Then Shō-ichi, sitting at the head of the table, urged me to sit at his left, and Haruko sat down on my left.

The kitchen, which had been renovated about ten years earlier, contained a four-burner stove with an oven, a sink, and a small refrigerator. The table and chairs with torn, green plastic seats filled the floor space, so that only by squeezing past them could one get to the dishes and the leftover food stored uncovered on shelves behind them. The kitchen in a country house is like an architectural afterthought, typically placed at ground level, unlike the rest of the house, which is raised and lined with tatami. Situated in the northeast corner of the house, it is the coldest, most isolated room, usually reserved exclusively for women and intended only for cooking and not as a place in which to eat. Traditional moral teachings instructed men never to enter the kitchen, which was woman's realm. Meals are usually served in the living room or in the guest room, but Shō-ichi and Haruko evidently preferred to eat in the kitchen, which could seat the six people who now made up their household.

The two children and Shō-ichi's mother, whom everyone called Obāsan (Grandmother), ate in silence; when he wanted more rice, Hisashi nudged his mother's sleeve with his bowl. Haruko frequently jumped up to refill rice bowls, pour tea, and serve seconds. In addition, every few minutes, like a subject under hypnosis, she would rise slowly from her seat, concentrating intensely on one of the several dozen flies that swarmed into the kitchen from the pigsty behind the house and buzzed relentlessly overhead. Raising her hands on each side of her victim, she would hold her breath and catch her prey in mid-air with a loud slap. Once she did so inches from my left ear.

Meanwhile, Shō-ichi attempted to converse with me in English, but his garbled pronunciation of the few words he knew was as difficult for me to understand as his Japanese. "Do you rike pashimon?" he asked, pointing to the plump, dark orange persimmon on the table. Later he wanted to know why so many Americans used the word "godem." He meant "Goddamn," a word he had heard frequently during the year he worked with Mexican migrants and dirt farmers in California.

Shō-ichi's efforts were met with teasing laughter by the children, whose jeers aroused in me a combination of irritation and mild embarrassment. Sitting through the ordeal of dinner—I do not remember what we ate—in the gloomy kitchen of this tense and uncommunicative family, I wondered whether I would be able to stay for one month, let alone half a year.

2
Haruko Takes Charge

DESPITE HARUKO's initial apprehensions that she would be unable to make me feel comfortable or even to feed me during my stay, she soon began to lavish on me the same devoted care she afforded her husband and children. First she organized my morning meals. After finding out what I liked to eat for breakfast, she arranged the same breakfast for me every day for the next six months. She prepared it early in the morning before she went out, leaving it for me to eat whenever I woke up, which was usually several hours later than anybody else in the family. Every morning I found a (cold) fried egg, instant coffee, a coffee cup and saucer next to a thermos of hot water, two slices of white bread, and homemade jam. One day, Haruko casually asked me if I drank milk, and before long the milkman began leaving a small bottle of milk for me.

Haruko soon began managing other aspects of my life as well. Every day, upon returning to my room, I would find one new item in it. One day it was a tin trunk for storing my clothes; another day, a few more nails on which to hang my clothes and a blue plastic basket to carry my clean underwear to the bath. Haruko assumed the tasks of washing, mending, and ironing my clothes, and as we grew more familiar with each other, she became my wardrobe mistress, advising me how many layers of underwear to don, which clothes flattered me and which did not, when it was time to leave a well-worn blouse in the laundry for washing, and how to wear my turtleneck wool sweater—I had been wearing it backwards for eighteen years, until Haruko, who knitted sweaters for the children, corrected me.

I could not fully explain Haruko's behavior toward me, nor could I reconcile it with her apparent unwillingness to make me welcome on the day of my arrival, but I suspected that her energetic mothering had to do with her discovery that I lacked a number of the practical skills, such as cooking and sewing, that are possessed almost universally by Japanese women. This realization of my helplessness, coupled with the fact that at the age of forty-two she was a number of years older than I, probably led her to assume toward me the maternal role she was accustomed to playing not only with her two children but also with her husband, whom she called Tō-chan, or Daddy. But my ascription of her behavior to a change in her attitude was only partly correct. Years later she told me that when I first arrived at her house, she had merely observed proper Japanese etiquette, which calls for hosts to make humble disclaimers, particularly when welcoming special guests, such as university professors. "If I had not wanted you to stay with us or if I had really felt that I could not handle the situation," she shrugged, "I would not have agreed to put you up in the first place. I was only being modest." At any rate, for whatever reasons, I was soon a recipient of the privileges as well as the obligations of family membership.

Haruko's sense of responsibility for me clearly extended well beyond the usual landlord-tenant or homeowner-boarder relationship practiced in the United States. The difference is, first of all, that Americans like contractual relationships; Japanese do not. Thus Haruko was loath to accept payment for my room and board; I was able to pay her only by leaving money in an envelope on the living-room table when she was out of the house. At the same time, Haruko was constitutionally incapable of observing any boundaries between herself and me. I never knew, for example, when she would burst into my room. "My husband gets angry with me for coming in without warning, but you don't mind, do you?" she would ask. "Is it all right?" was the only advance notice I got before she slid open the door to my room at ten o'clock one evening to offer me four rich pieces of cake (chocolate icing, whipped cream—an extravagant Japanese rendition of Viennese pastry) which she had bought for me in town. "Taste it. How is it?" I tried one-fourth of one slice. "Why don't you finish it? Don't you like it?"

For a long time I clung to the notion that I had certain inviolable rights of tenancy, for example to organize my room to suit my comfort and my tastes. Haruko, however, had no understanding of such rights. Once, I hit on the idea of dividing the quilts and mattresses in my room into two low piles, one right next to the other, and throwing a blanket over both, to form a kind of day bed, but while I was out of the room the two piles miraculously merged into one again. Several times I tried to remove the arrow and the framed documents that stood in the alcove, in order to create the aesthetic spareness I had always associated with the *tokonoma*, but each time I found them mysteriously replaced the next day.

Still, it was only after several months, in early March, that I realized the folly of thinking the room I occupied was truly mine. By then, despite the lack of furniture, I had managed to organize my papers and research materials into some sort of working order. I set up stacks of notes on the floor, in separate piles for each subject, and I spread out writing paper, camera equipment, letters, questionnaires, and other business on a low table in the corner. One day I returned home to find that Haruko had reassigned me to the narrow room in the front of the house that Yōko had originally occupied. In my absence, all my neatly arranged papers, including bills, university correspondence, and the telephone numbers and addresses of Japanese acquaintances, had been thrown "temporarily" into a carton and the carton shoved into the crammed closet. The systems I had devised for ordering my personal and professional life were smashed.

Backed up against the door of the closet, where my papers were now stored, was a display of fifty dolls arranged by Haruko to celebrate Girls' Day. The dolls, dressed in brightly colored Japanese clothing, sat on tiers that were covered with a red cloth on the table I had been using for my papers. Stunned, I asked Haruko how long the dolls would be there, and in disbelief heard her answer, "Until April 4th."

"April 4th?" I repeated, stupidly.

"Yes," Haruko replied, smiling.

"But Girls' Day is celebrated on March 3rd, isn't it?" I persisted, trying to negate the reality of the colossus that stood before me.

"No, it's celebrated here later than in Tokyo. I took out the dolls for the first time in several years. For you."

Dimly I began to see the humor of the situation. When I first arrived, I was a guest and Haruko had moved Yōko across the road to stay with her grandmother so that she would not disturb me. Increasingly, I had become a member of the family, and now I was ready to be moved to the room that used to be occupied by Yōko.

The symbol of my predicament was the chair I found in Yōko's old room. I used it to work at my "desk," the stubby surface of the sewing machine. It was a rickety chair too small for my seat; and the back of the chair came up only as far as the small of my back. How am I supposed to keep my balance, I wondered. But maybe that was the whole point. I had a strong tendency to balance myself—to organize my room like a study, and my life like lecture hours in a day. Such personal independence was impossible in this Japanese household, where all were expected to be flexible and cooperative.

From my earliest days in her house, Haruko regarded me, not as a tenant, but as someone whose status was halfway between that of a guest and that of a daughter, and since I shared in the life of the household, she felt that it was necessary and correct to take upon herself the responsibility not only for my comfort and well-being, but also for my appearance and conduct. Early in my stay, she bought me a set of long underwear, and when I seemed to be catching a cold, she went to the clinic in town for medicine. Her own cold preventive was a glass of homemade wine, which she drank every night before going to sleep, and she urged me to do the same. When I poured the wine, however, I discovered six dead flies floating in it. I switched to drinking whiskey, her husband's preference, and that seemed to satisfy her just as well.

My casual disregard for clothing and general physical appearance, however, exasperated her. Anticipating the rugged conditions of my rural environment, I had brought with me only my sturdiest clothing—proven survivors of hiking and camping trips over the last fifteen years. Obsessed with the need to stay warm, I had even packed a pair of booties recommended for Alaskan trappers.

Haruko, too, worried about keeping me warm. When the first snow fell on the valley in December, she dragged out an electric blanket and a heavy sweater for me. As chill winter winds blew across the rice plain and into the room through cracks in the wood, I wrote my journal entries wearing mittens that Haruko had knitted for me. But Haruko was equally worried about making me presentable to the outside world. What I wore indoors did not bother her except for the booties, which had fake leather soles and looked too much like shoes—and shoes are never worn inside a Japanese house. Once I stepped outside the entryway, however, I became fair game for her critical eye.

She paid strict attention to the distinctions between forms of clothing. *Hanten* (lightweight jackets) and *ponchi* (vests) were worn only in the house, whereas *haori* (also lightweight jackets) were put on over a kimono and worn outside the house, because they had a seamed edge running around the collar and down the front. You could not wear a *yukata* (a lightweight kimono) in winter; you could not wear red or pink after the age of forty; you could not wear dark green rain boots (they're for grandmothers).

Haruko was a fanatic on the subject of colors. As it happened, the practical clothes I had brought with me were in colors appropriate for women in their late forties and fifties—navy blue, dark green, brown, and gray. Haruko constantly urged me to wear brighter colors, advice I ignored until I interviewed a group of female factory workers who asked me my age. When I playfully urged them to guess, they said forty or fifty. I returned home dismayed. Haruko had an "I told you so" look on her face and repeated her suggestion about wearing bright greens and yellows, colors appropriate for women in their thirties.

Yet yellow was not always appropriate, as I learned one rainy day.

"I'm going to town. Be back soon," I called to Haruko.

"Don't rush," Haruko replied. "Be careful. . . . You're taking that umbrella?"

"Yes, since it's raining I thought I'd borrow it from the umbrella stand. Why? What's wrong?"

"It doesn't look right. The color—"

"What's wrong with this color? It's nice and bright. Drivers will be able to see me as I walk along the road."

Haruko paused. Then she ran into her bedroom, calling, "That color is for children. Here. Take this. A black one."

Although Haruko urged me to dress more attractively "in order to please your boyfriend," I suspected that she herself dressed for other women and not to attract the notice of men or even to please her husband. She often neglected to brush her hair, she picked her teeth in front of us, and she emerged from the toilet with her slacks still unbuttoned and her long underwear hanging out. "Japanese women notice externals," she said, "like what you wear or how you talk. You can be sure everybody has noticed the way Mrs. Kodama flutters her eyes when she talks." (Haruko imitated the fluttery eyes of an acquaintance.) "Their own eyes roam all over you when you talk. But my friends have remarked that you don't pay attention to such things. When they talk, you look right at them; your eyes don't wander. They admire this."

A few days later, Haruko was aghast to learn of a faux pas I had committed. I had absent-mindedly set out for the town library still wearing my *ponchi*, the yellow and pink wool vest she had knitted for me. From her anguish, I gathered my behavior was akin to appearing in public in a nightgown. Worse still, I had been met at the library by two newspaper reporters who had asked to interview me and take my picture, and under interrogation from Haruko I could not remember whether I had removed the *ponchi* for the picture.

"How can you not remember what you were wearing?" Haruko asked incredulously, conveying again the extreme importance she placed on one's appearance and performance in a public situation, but also indicating her veritable passion—one shared by other farm women—for clothes.

Haruko herself had an impressive collection of clothes, many of which she had made herself. Whenever she worked outside the house, she wore five to eight layers of clothing insulating her against the sun, insects, water, and cold. Dressed for winter, in a bulky assortment of long underwear, a blouse, a vest, a sweater, and a pair of *monpe* (baggy pantaloons), she weighed about 130 pounds; undressed, about ten pounds less. She owned a large assortment of Japanese and western work clothes in various styles: different kinds of footgear (rubber boots, clogs, sandals, slippers, and *tabi*—Japanese socks); varying lengths and weights of cotton underwear; accessories, such as long gloves, short gloves, scarves, hats, and face masks; kimonos with all the accessories (long slips, camisoles, *obi*, *obi* ties); handknit collars that buttoned under the chin to keep the neck and shoulders warm; and a jacket, a windbreaker, and slacks. For working in the fields, she donned long sleeves that were put on like gloves and covered her arms to the elbow, leaving all the fingers except the thumb exposed. Over these sleeves she wore rubber or wool gloves to protect her hands.

Bloated with clothing, like a child dressed for a snowstorm, Haruko nevertheless looked fetching in her work clothes. Though she worked side by side in the fields with men, she deferred to feminine fashion like all the other women in Bessho by wearing a dainty pink or white wraparound apron with ruffled edges, a white scarf wrapped around her neck, and a style of checkered bonnet then in vogue among the women. She also applied face powder before going to work in the fields, in order to protect her face from sunburn, fair skin being considered a mark of beauty in Japan. Bundled up in work clothes and wielding an iron hoe that was almost as tall as she was, she looked at once diminutive and tough, cute and competent, and her coy appearance belied the manual labor she was called upon to perform.

Western-style clothing, which she loved, was less flattering to her. On her trips to town, she wore brown slacks over several layers of underwear, a brown sweater, and a bulky jacket in a pepper-and-salt pattern, with big shoulder pads and a belt that made her look shorter and stockier than she was. Her handknit, round brown hat curled up at the edges and sat on her head like a bowler. Since she was slightly bowlegged, she rocked from side to side when she walked, and her ankle-high boots, which made her legs seem shorter than they really were, exaggerated the impression she gave of sinking into the ground.

No matter what she wore, however, she invariably reminded me of one of Snow White's dwarfs. Perhaps it was the mischievous way she laughed, wrinkling up her nose and opening her mouth wide to expose two silver teeth. The sound that emerged—more like a cackle —seemed to come from midway in her throat. Perhaps too this imp-ish quality had to do with her small stature (she was five feet tall) and her physical agility. I think it was also related to her unpredictability. Riding her motor scooter back from town (with me holding on be-hind her), she would suddenly stop, leap off, plunge into the cabbage patch along the road, and pull out a ripe cabbage to cook for dinner. If she asked whether I would like some persimmons and got a pos-itive response, she would hang a straw basket around her arm and shinny up the persimmon tree in front of the house.

I never knew from one day to another, or even from one hour to the next, where I would find her. One afternoon I returned home from an interview and, as I stood washing my hands at the sink, I was startled to hear her ask me, "How did it go today?" Her voice seemed to be coming from somewhere along the ground near my feet.

"Where are you?" I asked.

Without answering, she went on, "Did you get a lot of infor-mation?"

Feeling as though I were talking to a ghost, I responded, "Yes, lots—but where are you?"

"Here."

I turned around and looked down. Under the living room was a trap door leading to a crawl space, where Haruko sat on the floor holding a flashlight and sorting a pile of potatoes.

Despite her work outfits and her less than inviting work sites— pigsties, cabbage patches, crawl spaces—by virtue of being a woman, a wife, and a mother Haruko felt competent and, indeed, called upon to serve as a critic of ladies' and men's fashions. This was as much a part of her sphere of domestic responsibility as childrearing, cooking, and growing potatoes.

In addition to color, one other criterion underlying her fashion sense was cleanliness. She had a horror of dirt-stained clothing. My sneakers filled her with dismay, and she would not allow me to wear them on any formal occasion, such as a courtesy call paid on the mayor; she insisted I wear the only other pair of shoes I had brought—gum-soled, laced oxfords. Once, she hung on her husband's arm as he was leaving the house, dressed in his work clothes, and begged him to change into a clean shirt because "You smell like a pigsty!"

Yet Haruko's virtual dread of dirt did not betoken a concern with cleanliness in general. As far as I could tell, the sink where we washed our hands and kept our toothbrushes was cleaned only on New Year's Day. Dishes were washed in the kitchen sink in cold water, and dirty pots and plates were left to pile up on the floor or wherever there was a place in the kitchen to put them. And whereas Haruko's Japanese-style clothes were stored with infinite care—folded in a prescribed way, wrapped in paper, laid flat in drawers, and preserved in camphor—there was absolutely no sense of care or order in the way food items were stored. Different pieces of leftover food were crammed haphazardly into the refrigerator, and other food items were piled in paper bags and boxes squeezed into cupboards, stuffed into every available space.

Stains rather than unsanitary conditions bothered Haruko. Thus she would leap up in alarm whenever soy sauce was accidentally spilled on the blue-and-white checkered plastic tablecloth and seize a dirty rag to wipe it up. And though she could kill a fly in her hands, brush it off, and continue eating, she would recoil in horror at a dirt mark on my sweater, insisting that I remove the sweater immediately so she could wash it.

Haruko's notions of right and wrong went beyond clothing. She presided over a multitude of social forms and rules of etiquette that she fiercely enforced in transactions outside the family. Some of these struck me as arbitrary, much like the western practice of placing the fork on the left-hand side of the plate—convenient only for left-handed eaters—and the knife and spoon on the right. I remembered as a child memorizing the correct positions of salad forks and soup spoons and water glasses, rules I continue to adhere to: I feel uncomfortable if a knife rests where the fork should be. I imagine this is the feeling Haruko experienced when I unknowingly violated one of the canons of taste she had been taught. Thus she reminded me to turn my chopsticks around when serving myself from a common dish; to place food from a serving dish onto my plate, and not directly into my mouth; and to peel a pear before and not after slicing it. She also insisted that I learn the proper way to wrap a package, address an envelope, and fold a kimono.

Considering her casual and even blunt manner around the house and her straightforward way of speaking, it seemed at first out of character if not hypocritical of Haruko to belabor these fine points with me. Though I could appreciate that certain social situations dictated the observance of the prescribed formalities, Haruko sometimes seemed overzealous in her efforts to tutor me in the ways of Japanese polite society, to teach me manners that she and Shō-ichi had discarded long ago and did not bother to teach their own children.

Traditional Japanese etiquette requires hosts to extend certain courtesies to their guests, for example to ply them with food and drink, and requires guests, in turn, to practice *enryo*, or reserve, politely declining until their hosts strenuously insist. Knowing whether the other party is being sincere or merely polite takes a certain amount of discernment; it is sometimes necessary to accept even when one does not want to, just as it is necessary to offer when one wishes not to. Haruko and Shō-ichi were actually impatient with such subtle forms of interaction; when Haruko observed these niceties, she did so in an unconvincing way, as though she were a tape recording, and Shō-ichi, on at least one occasion, chided his mother for pressing food on a guest, saying, "Let her take whatever she wants by herself!"

Yet Haruko seemed to feel compelled to transmit some of these social conventions to me.

"Give Auntie some of that fruit," she instructed me one day.

I offered our elderly guest the fruit, though she already had a full plate of food in front of her.

"I already have some," she said, pointing to the pile of fruit on her crowded plate.

"Give Auntie some fruit," Haruko repeated.

It seemed cruel to force more food on the old woman.

"She says she has enough," I replied.

Everyone at the table laughed. The old woman slowly made room on her plate and took some more.

Haruko was far more than the official arbiter of taste and the authority on social propriety. She was Superintendent of Daily Life, the Office Manager, the Inspector-General, the checker of everything that entered and left the house. In charge of Shipping and Receiving, from the entryway she examined clothes, packages, and incoming and outgoing mail. She soon knew how much mail I was getting and from whom; all postcards written in Japanese were treated with as much privacy as a newspaper. "I see Mrs. Ishikawa received your last letter," she would say, handing me a postcard from Mrs. Ishikawa. Haruko was the Camp Mother, the Head Counselor in charge of five campers—their laundry, their stomachs, their education, and their general health and deportment. She barked orders all day, like a Master Sergeant. When sick or resting, she called out commands from bed, behind the closed doors of her bedroom: "Hisashi, go to bed; it's late." Or, "Yōko, take your bath!" Or, "Daddy" (to her husband), "don't forget to call Mr. Seike." And then, if unheeded, she repeated the orders more urgently, "Hisashi, Hisashi, fast, go to bed!" If I sneezed in the middle of the night, she called from her own bed, "Do you need another blanket?"

Whereas on the one hand Haruko worked slavishly for us, on the other she controlled our lives and guided them, precisely because her devotedness made all of us heavily dependent on her physical and psychological support. A human computer, Haruko kept track of everybody's work responsibilities, deadlines, and appointments: she remembered Yōko's school money, Hisashi's gloves, a clean handkerchief for her husband. She reminded me of daily tasks I needed to accomplish: Buy film for your camera. Don't forget to pick up a train schedule. Did you write your mother? . . .

Above all, Haruko felt responsible for helping me complete my research project. Every night during my first week in her household, as we sat around the *kotatsu* drinking our cold-preventives, she asked me what my "objective" was, and every night she managed to draw from me a more concrete statement of it. Little by little she penetrated the wall of vagueness I had constructed, until one evening I blurted out the truth: I was there to study Japanese family life from the inside. I intended, I told her, to write a humanistic account centered on women—their work, their relationships, and their emotions. I wanted to know exactly what it was like living in a Japanese family, including the conflicts and the problems. Moreover, I planned to keep a diary, take photographs, and publish my account.

To my vast relief, Haruko was delighted, and she offered to help in any way she could. As the weeks wore on, she served variously as my press secretary, informant, agent, and, finally, co-author, writing a thirty-six-page autobiography to add to the material I was collecting on my own. Knowing that her life story might appear in print one day, she became even more concerned than I was about the progress I was making. "You're never going to finish your interviews if you sleep so late in the morning," she would say, sharply; or, "If you don't *ask* people for their pictures, you're not going to have enough illustrations."

As her days grew busier, Haruko often forgot that her life was the subject of a book, and I never once doubted that Haruko was being anything other than herself—spontaneous, exasperating, loving, smothering, perceptive, anxious, energetic, and totally human. Whether I could continue to be myself in my new environment was another matter, and one that caused both me and my hosts not a little consternation.

3
Entering the Community

THE QUESTION of my social status within the community troubled Haruko from the very beginning of my stay. One day shortly after my arrival she asked if family members and guests should be instructed to call me Sensei (Teacher), but I hastily declined the honor with the average American's disdain for titles and for the superior status they implied. If my goal was to penetrate the heart of the Japanese farm woman, I reasoned, I certainly should not go around putting on airs. It would be hard enough breaking down the excessive respect the Japanese customarily gave Americans and guests. Besides, I did not want to make the subjects of my interviews and observations self-conscious in my presence. It would be best, I decided, not to reveal my purposes to anybody else.

My misguided humility cost me weeks of frustration. What I interpreted as unfriendliness or shyness on the part of the two hundred permanent residents of the hamlet was, in retrospect, uncertainty about who I was and how I should be treated—an extremely important consideration for Japanese living in close daily contact with each other. Moreover, by concealing the purpose of my stay, I was depriving myself of a role to play and, in the inhabitants' eyes, of adult status. Once the people of Bessho knew who I was and why I was there, they were more willing to talk with me as a *sensei* and to help me gather the information I needed.

Haruko assisted me by contacting local newspapers and suggesting that they do a story about me. What prompted her was a newspaper article about a nineteen-year-old American college student living in the prefecture for a one-month work-study program. Haruko thought it shocking that I was overlooked in favor of somebody with fewer credentials; and, on her own, with her characteristic zeal in organizing my life, she arranged for a newspaper to interview me, neglecting to tell me her scheme until one hour before the scheduled interview.

The newspaper interview led to requests for interviews by other local newspapers; public appearances before women's groups, the PTA, the Young Farmers' Club, and a junior high school English club; and inquiries from two television stations. If Haruko was delighted, I was dismayed: I had become a prefectural celebrity. But I had also become a known commodity, and this was reassuring to everyone I met. I found it was no longer necessary to conceal from the people I was interviewing the tools of my trade—notebooks, dictionaries, and a list of interview questions. Instead of memorizing what people had told me and staying up for hours afterward writing it all down before I forgot it, I took notes in front of my respondents, asked them to repeat difficult sentences, and even stopped to look up unfamiliar words in my dictionary. "We feel honored that an American professor would be interested in our lives," an eighty-year-old man told me.

I had originally feared that the knowledge that I planned to publish an account of my experiences in rural Japan might inhibit frank discussion, especially among women unaccustomed to speaking freely even with their neighbors, much less with strangers. I found, however, that if I appeared under "official" auspices, sponsored by the principal of the local junior high school, for example, or a former Diet representative from the area, who urged the women gathered for my benefit to "tell Sensei anything she wants to know," the women complied.

By agreeing to give a talk before a local school or the PTA, I could legitimately ask a favor in return from the school principal or the PTA president who had solicited my appearance. That favor was an opportunity to talk with a small group of farm women or to administer a questionnaire I had prepared on work and wages. The local leaders had impressive influence: once, I handed a junior high school principal in a remote mountain village ten copies of the seven-page questionnaire and he returned all ten the very next morning, filled out by the mothers of the students he had sent them home with. Though I felt guilty about using people in authority to make demands upon busy farm women, everybody, including the women, appeared more comfortable this way—a *certified* way—whereas when I approached strangers directly, they seemed understandably suspicious and ill at ease.

The trouble with officially sponsored appearances, however, was that they were invariably treated like the visits of a ranking dignitary. My appearance at a public function occasioned elaborate preparations. No matter how small the gathering or how remote its location, certain rituals of good form were mandatory. A driver, usually wearing white gloves, was sent to fetch me. Several male officials greeted me upon my arrival. While I sat making light conversation in their offices, a young woman inevitably appeared with green tea and pastries. After a few minutes, I was escorted to another room, where the local Women's Guild members were seated, waiting for me. I was placed upon a stage, or seated on the floor Japanese style, at a distance of at least several feet from my audience. I was formally introduced and expected to give a talk. Usually my topic was a quasi-humorous comparison of the differences between American and Japanese marriages. Mention of the divorce rate in the United States invariably brought gasps, and the women were amused by my description of the logistics of visitation rights, whereby mothers and fathers visited or played host to their own children. But the question-and-answer period reminded me of the familiar classroom experience of the teacher who must urge the reticent students to "open up." The situation was far too intimidating.

To help me get in touch with farm women, Haruko offered to introduce me to her female relatives or to take me to her Women's Guild meetings. The results were usually disappointing. Her eager-beaver manner made me and everybody else feel self-conscious. Also, she heartily disapproved of my questionnaire, finding it too impersonal. When I left the survey questions at home, however, and instead tried to engage people in informal discussion, she became impatient with me for not knowing exactly what I wanted to ask, asking it, and leaving. Haruko was definitely a doer.

Once, at a Women's Guild meeting, Haruko decided on her own to encourage a candid discussion of sexual attitudes, but her frankness and nervous chatter stunned the ladies present and left them stony-faced and embarrassed.

"We talk freely about everything with her," she told them. "For example, she wanted to know how Japanese couples show affection, since they always act like strangers to each other in public."

A few titters from the audience.

"So, I said, 'We show our affection in bed.' "

More titters, followed by silence.

On another occasion, driven by nervous energy, Haruko talked endlessly and recklessly in an effort to get the women to respond to my questions. Like a comedian warming up an audience, she relayed my impressions of farm life, including candid observations I had made to her about other women I had interviewed. Her revelations naturally inhibited the audience all the more, and she ended up talking to the air.

Even on less formal occasions, such as a hamlet feast or a gathering at the house of a relative, I was treated as a guest and separated from the very people I wanted to meet. A guest, even if female, was seated near the head of the table—the end closest to the alcove—together with all the men. Women in white aprons clustered together at the other end of the table, near the door leading to the kitchen. Though I might protest that I had come to Japan to study farm women's work, and therefore preferred to sit with women or stay in the kitchen, my protestations would go unheeded, as the host urged me to drink more *sake* and eat more food.

I finally decided that my best resource was private interviews with one woman at a time. This technique had its disadvantages too. If the woman was young, her mother-in-law was nearby and expected to be included in my visit. The older woman's presence effectively eliminated any opportunity for candor, especially since an important area of conflict in rural Japan is that between daughter-in-law and mother-in-law.

In the wintertime, when the family huddled around the *kotatsu*, the single source of heat, it became perforce necessary to conduct a group interview. Group interviews were often surprisingly revealing. My asking a woman, in the presence of her husband, whether she felt exploited by him, for example, produced a variety of reactions, from merry joking to serious discussion, and once a heated exchange broke out when I asked a young woman if she wanted her husband to help her more with the housework. "No, not with the housework," she replied, "but with the children. Or, if only he would just leave me alone when I'm in the kitchen, instead of asking me to bring him an ashtray."

Through Shō-ichi's many acquaintances in the county, I received invitations for home stays with other families, where I had opportunities to meet women from different backgrounds and in various economic and household circumstances. Eventually my problem became not one of being integrated into village and family life, but one of getting myself extricated from the many obligations incumbent upon me as a member of my new family.

It was first of all necessary to pay official calls on some of the community's dignitaries, including the high school principal and the head of the township. In preparation for such visits, Haruko ordered name cards on which appeared, for the sake of courtesy and convenience, not only my name but my university affiliation and the Utsunomiyas' address and telephone number printed in Japanese. At the same time, Shō-ichi instructed me to speak in English—"Simple English," Haruko interjected—to anyone who knew even a few words of the language, and especially to the high school English teacher, who would undoubtedly be waiting for us when we visited the principal. "You'll make him look good," he explained.

Shō-ichi and I waited for the first rainy day—the farmer's only holiday—to pay a call on the high school principal. When we arrived at the school, the English teacher, as we anticipated, was waiting for us. The principal's office was furnished with leather chairs arranged in a square with a low table in the center. A female clerk quickly entered and placed bowls of green tea before us. There was a moment of silence as the principal and I exchanged name cards and bows. The principal said a few words of welcome in Japanese, and then the teacher spoke a few hesitant words in English. I complimented him on his fluency.

Later that day, Shō-ichi beamed as he described my performance to Haruko. "She even praised the English teacher's English in front of the rest of us," he said. Both agreed that I was getting better at the game of social intercourse, Japanese style, which often seemed to involve suppressing one's real feelings and opinions for the sake of etiquette, group harmony, and "status" or "face," two words Shō-ichi used frequently. Shō-ichi reminded me to speak in English if I was invited to the teacher's house for dinner, explaining, "You'll raise his status in his wife's eyes." He added that this was a particularly important consideration for young couples.

The matter of English conversational skills was a peculiarly sensitive one for Shō-ichi and his friends. Among the men in his circle of rural acquaintances—men who had not been abroad and had never associated with foreigners—saying a few words in English, especially if they had been drinking, became a kind of jocular challenge. Meeting me, one man in the group would shout excitedly in English, "Stand up, stand up!" patting the seat cushion next to him to indicate I should please sit down. Such efforts were invariably greeted with shouts of laughter and teasing from other men in the group, just as Shō-ichi's efforts to say a few words in English to me on the first night I ate dinner with his family had provoked jeers from his children.

Having heard other foreigners describe their frustrations in trying to communicate with the Japanese in either Japanese or English, I began to suspect a national neurosis created by the numerous emotions associated with speaking to a foreigner. Nervousness, a feeling of inferiority, uneasiness lest the foreigner prove to be unfamiliar with the rules of Japanese social intercourse or unable to understand the Japanese speaker, a genuine desire to accommodate the foreigner by speaking in his or her language—all these emotions may have entered into the remarkably consistent response to my presence. Knowing English, at any rate, is an important qualification for membership in the Japanese elite and is therefore one way for Japanese to impress each other. Thus, whenever Shō-ichi introduced me to any of the young farmers in the community who had lived, however briefly, in the United States, he reminded me to "make them look good" by speaking to them in English. My presence at social gatherings was a cause of anxiety both for me and for my fellow guests, especially when we conversed in English: "Did she understand you?" someone would ask, or, "Did you understand her?" The same questions were asked when we spoke in Japanese, and introductions became a painful, if predictable, ordeal, not helped by my own faltering attempts to comprehend the local dialect, with its peculiar pronunciation and inflections and its sometimes unfamiliar vocabulary and verb forms.

My idea of being a participant-observer, I soon realized with chagrin, had been hopelessly naive. The objects of my study were themselves observing me, and rather than slipping silently into the environment like the proverbial fly on the wall, I found myself the center of attention wherever I went.

When I was introduced at any social gathering, people's reactions seemed designed to establish my foreignness, to set me apart as an object of exotic interest. Somebody would wonder aloud whether I could eat Japanese food or use chopsticks. Although Haruko and Shō-ichi explained that they spoke to me in Japanese, people discussed me as though I were not there. When I tried to speak, in order to assure people that I could communicate with them, however feebly, my responses were received with looks of incomprehension and murmurs of "She probably doesn't understand," or they were excitedly repeated: "She says the fruit tastes good."

Racial differences were uppermost in everybody's mind. Once, during a noontime feast following a session of rice-threshing, the men in the work group, who had not met me before, engaged in joking and hazing much as they might have with a new bride in the hamlet, commenting on my looks and asking me to guess their ages. The women joined in, asking me how much I weighed and how tall I was. "Her skin is whiter than ours," said one man. "And her eyes are blue. Do all foreign women have dark hair?" Jokes with sexual innuendoes directed at me were greeted by laughter from the men and blushes from the women.

"You're a novelty," Haruko said, deflecting my implied criticism of these sessions, which made me feel like a horse on the auction block or like a child. "You're something rare." Haruko and Shō-ichi appeared to enjoy the attention focused on me, and they would praise me lavishly in front of the others. But even they grew tired of answering the same questions. "Does she use the Japanese-style toilet?" was a question Shō-ichi heard so many times that he finally learned to reply, "No, she is waiting until she goes home."

Once these initiation ceremonies—as I tried to view them—were over, and the issue of my foreignness publicly explored, there was little further notice of it among people who had met me, though there remained an abiding, neighborly interest in my comings and goings, and as one might expect of any close community, members of the hamlet seemed to know about my activities almost before I did. "When are you leaving for Tokyo?" a hamlet woman asked one day as she passed me only minutes after I had purchased the train tickets for my trip.

Curiously, nobody thought to introduce me to the police, even though local units of the Japanese national police organization are scrupulous about keeping track of all residents within their area of responsibility. After I had lived in Bessho for three months, a police inspector who was new to the region came to the house and, ignoring me altogether, asked Shō-ichi who I was, why I was there, and how long I planned to remain. A tall, thin, attractive man with an urbane charm and a slightly unctuous manner, he soon returned to headquarters where, he later told us, he learned for the first time that Shō-ichi was a local leader who was much respected in the community. He immediately telephoned to apologize for insufficient *aisatsu* (greetings), and came back to the house one evening a few days later to offer a gift of rich pastry.

Haruko met him at the door and explained that Shō-ichi and I were at a meeting of the *shigin* club at a neighbor's house, where

about fifteen hamlet residents gathered once a week to practice clas-
sical Chinese songs. I do not know whether she offered to escort him
through the unlit pathways of Bessho to the neighbor's house or
whether he asked her to, but all at once we saw him squeezing into
the crowded circle of singers, asking if he could join the group. He
turned out to have a booming baritone voice.

Afterward, he returned to the Utsunomiya house and stayed until
eleven o'clock. A few days later he returned again, this time, he said,
to chat with Shō-ichi about politics and to ask his opinion on the
probable outcome of the upcoming gubernatorial election. After this
visit, the family had no further contact with him.

As my circle of acquaintances expanded from Haruko and Shō-
ichi to include the many people I met directly or indirectly through
them, my chain of indebtedness likewise grew. It was virtually impossible to turn down requests for favors. It was even impossible to
delay beyond one day doing the favor. Giving and receiving favors is
the stuff of Japanese life, the cement of social relations. Exacting favors is the "real soul of the Japanese," as one farmer, flushed with
whiskey, told me. "The person you help has *giri*: he is much obliged
to you. He wants to repay your kindness. He feels *giri*. If my friend
gets sick and has no money, I take my money and give it to him."

Requests made of me were usually modest and invariably meant
doing what I did best, namely, performing as an American. When
guests came, I was expected to sit with them and make conversation.
At first it seemed a simple way for me to repay the many kindnesses
I had received from the Utsunomiya family, as well as a convenient
means of meeting people. But because Shō-ichi had a vast network
of friends and acquaintances, and because hardly anybody in the
county, with the exception of some of the young male farmers, had
ever met a foreigner, I was soon on call at all hours of the day and
night.

Sometimes I was not consulted about the commitments made on
my behalf. Once, when I returned from a full day of interviewing and
was looking forward to resting alone in my room, Haruko announced that we were all going to her friend's home for dinner be-

cause the friend's son was home from high school and wanted to meet me. Another day, I heard Obāsan say over the telephone, "Yes, she's home," and then hang up.

"Who was that?" I asked.

"Mr. Itō."

"What did he want?"

"He's coming over to see you."

"Me? Now? Who is he?"

"I didn't ask."

"But I'm getting ready to go to bed!"

"Oh. I suppose I should have asked you first."

I stayed up waiting for Mr. Itō. He never arrived. The next morning Haruko burst into my room while I was still asleep. "Wake up! There is somebody to see you!" It was the mysterious Mr. Itō, one of Shō-ichi's numerous friends, asking me to write out a check for him in American dollars in exchange for Japanese yen. He wanted to write to the United States to register the American pedigree of his dog.

At other times, virtual strangers would drop by, uninvited, to see me. Once two men Shō-ichi had met earlier in the day at a wedding, who had read about me in a newspaper article, arrived unexpectedly after dinner. Drunk from the afternoon festivities, they tripped over each other entering the living room, and when they saw me they began shouting in pidgin English. "Teacha, teacha," one said, while the other one shook my hand vigorously. Meanwhile Shō-ichi, who had himself had his share of drink, quickly fell asleep on the floor, leaving Haruko and me no choice but to entertain the men by ourselves for the next two hours. The men insisted that I drink with them and kept trying to refill my glass. One of them dropped the bottle he was pouring and spilled whiskey over me, the table, and the tatami. The other man pumped my hand again. Finally, I followed Haruko into the kitchen and pleaded with her to get rid of the men or allow me to excuse myself and go to bed. Haruko, as always, tried to humor me, but urged, "Just a little longer."

Experiences such as these were balanced by the unfailing generosity and promptness with which other people, some of whom I had never met, might respond to my needs and interests. The drivers who magically appeared in the entryway to take me to other hamlets, the families who gave me lodging overnight and bought instant coffee for my breakfast the next morning, the couple who allowed me to attend their wedding and photograph them—it was impossible to keep track of all these strangers who, as friends or acquaintances of Shō-ichi's, put themselves at my disposal. There was hardly anything I was expected to do either for myself or by myself. The only appropriate response to all this good care, this secure second childhood, was gratitude, and yet a more frequent and abiding feeling was irritability, coupled with guilt. The strain of meeting new people, of having to interpret their dialect, and of having to make my own sentences intelligible to them began to take its toll.

Family members were not only aware of my feelings, but even sympathized with them. After the evening spent with the two drunken men, Shō-ichi apologized, explaining that he had not invited them: they had said they were coming, and he could not tell them not to. At lunch the same day, Obāsan said tactfully, "It was bothersome last night, wasn't it? Sensei had to talk to the guests."

Haruko tried to help by taking my part against the many people who wanted me to teach English to their children. "You can't waste your time," she said. "After all, you didn't come here to teach English. Just tell them, 'I'm sorry, but I'm busy.' "

Sanction for such straightforward refusals did not apply to her own close friends and relatives, however. One invitation I could not decline came from Hisashi's sixth-grade teacher, who wanted me to talk to his class.

"If you go, you'll raise Hisashi's status among his classmates," Haruko said. "If you don't go, both Hisashi and his teacher will be shamed."

"But what can I say to a class of twelve-year-olds?" I asked, sounding no more than twelve years old myself.

"Just tell them how hard you studied when you were young. It doesn't have to be much. Just show your face," she coaxed.

I explained that being the center of attention made me feel uncomfortable.

"No, no. It's not that at all!" Haruko exclaimed. "It's just that the only Americans anyone has ever known were military people. Japan was defeated by the Americans."

"It's more than that," Shō-ichi interrupted. "Japanese have only known American soldiers, strolling arm and arm with Japanese women. But you are *erai* [important], more cultured, high class."

"People are pleased by how kind you are," Haruko interjected, "the way you bow and say hello in Japanese to everybody you see—"

"And," Shō-ichi added, "America is ahead of Japan, more advanced—"

"But," I tried again, "I don't like being *erai*."

Haruko looked puzzled.

"You're not a movie star," Shō-ichi said, sympathetically.

"I'll write the talk for you," Haruko offered, and she did.

In such situations, I began to feel almost as a Japanese child might have felt in resisting its parents' wishes. For I owed a great deal to Haruko and Shō-ichi, and whenever I gave way to my westerner's compulsion to assert my rights, I was beset by feelings of childishness and guilt, but, above all, of obligation. It is precisely this strong sense of obligation that characterizes the feelings of Japanese children toward their parents, and it is most likely inculcated in them by the same kind of total care and sensitive anticipation of needs that I had myself received from Haruko and Shō-ichi. The obverse—"selfish" assertion of one's own will, and unwillingness to extend oneself for others—is roundly discouraged. In the kindnesses bestowed on me by the family and by others in the community, I sensed the force of social pressures bending and shaping me to Japanese society.

It was frequently hard to judge whether requests for favors were legitimate within the context of Japanese society. As I considered the request of Hisashi's sixth-grade teacher, I wonder whether as a *gaijin*, a foreigner, I had simply come to be perceived as a valuable resource and, falling outside the culture, could be exploited. Such questions were academic, however. In effect, I had no choice; I had to acquiesce. The real problem became one of learning how to submerge my will gracefully, something the Japanese learn to do by the time they have reached adulthood.

I received similar requests from other teachers. The very next day, in fact, shortly before dinnertime, the high school English teacher dropped by, uninvited. He had called first to ask if I was home and Haruko, busy cooking supper, had neglected to warn me he was coming. Haruko nervously led him into my room, behaving with her best company manners.

The English teacher was grim and unsmiling. He wore a dark gray tweed suit, a white shirt, a dark tie, and black-rimmed glasses. In rapid succession he requested my appearance at the high school festival, asked me to tape-record six hours of English lessons, and ordered me to move into his house beginning in January so that he could practice English. His simple English sentences made him sound ruder than he had intended: "We want you to record English. Do you agree?" I bristled. I tried to be generous and selfless. I conjured up the sweet, ever-smiling face of all the Japanese women I had met over the last fifteen years, their graciousness, their patience. I reminded myself of the importance of furthering Japanese-American cultural exchange. I forced a smile.

Haruko came in with tea and urged our guest to make himself comfortable. The teacher, looking taut-faced and pale, relaxed slightly. We talked about the difficulties of learning a foreign language without having native speakers to talk to. "I understand the problems you face in trying to teach English," I said. "I'll be happy to tape some lessons for you. I have my own tape recorder, so I can easily do it here."

We talked some more. Finally, I sneaked a look at my watch. Thirty minutes had passed. It was six-thirty.

"Well," I said, heartily. "It was so nice of you to come, and I shall try to attend your festival."

He continued sitting.

"And, ah, since the family here eats dinner at about six . . ."

He understood. As he left, Haruko fell on her knees at the entryway, thanking him over and over again for coming.

The Utsunomiya household,
New Year's Day, 1975. Left to
right: Hisashi, Yōko, Obāsan,
Haruko, Shō-ichi.

Haruko dressed for
a summer festival.

Yōko and Shō-ichi.

At the dinner table, I gave vent to my anger.

"That man! He was ordering me around like a slave. Isn't it rude to visit without being invited? Especially at dinnertime?"

Haruko interpreted my words as criticism of her.

"I'm sorry. I should have told you he was coming. He probably ate before he came." And taking my side, she added cynically, "A proper Japanese would smile and bow and endure, even if he stayed until ten o'clock." Here she assumed a mock smile, wrinkling her eyes and nodding her head up and down. "If you hadn't said anything, he would have stayed until at least seven o'clock. But since you are outside the family, it's all right. My husband couldn't say such things. I couldn't say such things."

But, of course, I was a part of the family, and therefore I had to help them fulfill their social obligations. I couldn't be rude to a man who might be their daughter's English teacher next year. By the same token, I could not very well refuse the junior high school principal's request that I put in an appearance at his school, especially when the invitation was issued in person by the principal himself, who surprised the Utsunomiya family one morning at breakfast by appearing in the entryway of their house. Unsmiling, he stood there in the early morning chill, elegantly dressed in a western two-piece brown suit with a brown fox-fur draped over his shoulders. I did what I knew I had to do. "Yes, yes," I said, bowing. "I would be happy to come to your school."

I would like to believe that I was reformed after this time, but there were many incidents of backsliding. Sensing my restlessness when forced to sit crosslegged or on my knees on the floor for several hours, eating, drinking, and conversing, Shō-ichi remarked sympathetically that I suffered from "burning seat." I overheard Haruko worriedly describe to my Japanese friend, who visited from Tokyo, how I would set up interviews and meetings with people and then try to get out of them. She also worried about my propensity for sleep—one of the few activities that guaranteed solitude and warmth.

The town of Unomachi helped rescue the situation. In the small public library or in one of the four dimly lit coffee shops, individual privacy was respected, and the taste of urban anomie, like the bitter espresso brew, was bracing. Further release from the strain of human interaction came from jogging in late afternoon to the railroad track and back, though before long I was accompanied by two eight-year-old Bessho girls who had befriended me. Haruko's tasty evening meals, a nightly English tutorial for Yōko that allowed me to use my own language while fulfilling some of my obligations to Haruko, who had suggested it, and Shō-ichi's warm, tranquil temperament were additional balms, so soothing that I began to dread leaving the haven of the Utsunomiya home for the various overnight trips that had been planned for me in other parts of the countryside.

One evening, at the end of my first month in Bessho, as Shō-ichi, Haruko, and I sat around the *kotatsu* in what had become a nightly routine of after-dinner conversation, I told them that I would talk to the junior high school students, appear before their son's sixth-grade class, and tape the high school teacher's English lesson, but that I did not want to live in the English teacher's house. "I want to stay here." In the silence that followed, I suddenly realized that, despite the tensions, after only four weeks I had grown comfortable with Haruko and Shō-ichi. Their home had become home for me, though I could not pinpoint the exact moment when they and I had changed in each other's eyes—when we had lost our mutual anxieties. Later that evening, Haruko, sensing the same change, said lightly, but gently, as if in passing, that she felt as though I were her child, and that she and her husband would feel lonely after I returned to the United States.

In this broad and ambivalent twilight zone between adoptive daughter and professional academic, I carried out my research and dwelt in the Utsunomiya household for the next five months.

PART II
Farm Family

4
Haruko and Shō-ichi

HARUKO FIRST MET her future husband in 1949, in the home of her uncle, who lived in the hamlet adjoining Bessho and was married to Shō-ichi's older sister. Both had gone to the uncle's house to help with the rice harvest. Haruko had just graduated from high school at the time and Shō-ichi thought she was "very cute," but they did not see each other again for another three years. By then, Shō-ichi's father had died and everyone was urging him to get married. There were several young women he liked, but he remembered Haruko, and his brother-in-law kept praising her to him, saying, "She's got a good head, she's good in arithmetic, and she's a hard worker." That Haruko was related to him through his brother-in-law made the match seem more desirable and helped Shō-ichi, then twenty-three years old, work up a passionate love for this twenty-year-old girl he barely knew.

Although the two saw each other at the local Youth Club meetings, they did not go out on dates. Haruko did not care much for Shō-ichi, because he did not dress well or "make a good appearance," though she did appreciate his seriousness and "honest, pure character." He, however, was madly in love: "My heart would pound whenever I saw her," he recalled. His romantic attraction to her, the encouragement of neighbors and relatives, and Haruko's practical attainments made him all the more determined to win her hand.

One day Shō-ichi startled Haruko at a Youth Club meeting by begging her to marry him. When she hesitated, he went alone to her father, whom he had never met, and boldly asked for permission to marry her. Since marriages were customarily arranged by go-betweens in accordance with the elaborate procedures prescribed by etiquette, Shō-ichi's behavior was highly irregular; Haruko was convinced he had become literally crazy with love for her. Her parents believed that a young man so eager to have their daughter as a wife would make a good husband. Nevertheless, they had reservations.

Their doubts centered on the young man's *iegara*, his family's status—the most important consideration in arranging marriages in Japan. A woman ideally married into a family whose social and economic position was slightly better than her own. Although Haruko's family were not rich, they owned two and one-half acres of paddy land—more than Shō-ichi's family—and thirty acres of forest land, making them one of the four or five most prosperous households in the hamlet.

Yet it was not the prospect of being a farmer's wife or even a poor farmer's wife that made Haruko hesitate: from an early age, she had been expected to help farm her family's land. A more serious drawback was Shō-ichi's position within his family. He was the eldest son in a family of seven children, two other children having died in infancy. He was only twenty years old when his father died, leaving him head of the household. Two of his sisters were already married, but three younger brothers and a younger sister were still at home, and he was now responsible for their welfare and for his forty-six-year-old widowed mother. By marrying the first son and heir of a farm family, Haruko would have to live with her husband's brothers and sisters until they married and with her husband's mother until she died.

Friction between mother-in-law and daughter-in-law would be inevitable. The Japanese household traditionally has just one housewife: only when the mother-in-law retires from family affairs or dies can the bride give up the status of daughter-in-law and become the woman of the house. If Haruko married Shō-ichi, she would not enjoy the independence of women who marry second or third sons and establish their own residences; instead she would be under the supervision of her husband's mother.

Wise in the ways of human affairs, Haruko's grandmother predicted that although Shō-ichi was a sincere person, Haruko would not have an easy life with him. Haruko herself was neither in love with him, nor did she dislike him. She was more attracted to another man, but in those days, she recalled, "It was considered shameful for a woman to express her love for a man. The man customarily voiced interest in a woman, and the woman was supposed to accept. Shō-ichi's ardent proposal gradually moved me. Hesitating at first, I finally decided that since I was short and not exceptionally pretty, I might not be able to do much better. My husband was so ardent, my family agreed to accept his marriage proposal, thinking that I might be happy after all with a man who was so serious. Ten years later, I learned that three different men had wanted to marry me, but had deferred to Shō-ichi because he had spoken for me first."

In the absence of an official go-between, Haruko's uncle (Shō-ichi's brother-in-law) served as marriage broker, bringing betrothal presents from Shō-ichi's house. These included a cash gift of thirty dollars, placed in an envelope tied with red and gold ties to which were attached three small, paper-covered wire figures of a crane, a tortoise, and a pine tree—traditional symbols of longevity. They did not have a formal betrothal ceremony. The uncle simply telephoned Haruko's family the day before, saying he was coming, and when he arrived he presented the gifts with the conventional words "Please accept these and keep them for a long time." Haruko's family prepared a dinner of *sake* and fish, and that was the extent of the engagement celebration.

After the engagement was announced, the couple dated briefly before Shō-ichi went to the United States on a farmer-training program. He spent one year working on potato farms in Arizona and California and writing romantic letters back home to his fiancée. One week before Shō-ichi's return to Japan, Haruko's nineteen-year-old sister was found dead of a cerebral hemorrhage, and partly as a result of the physical and emotional strain of the months that followed Haruko contracted tuberculosis and was hospitalized for half a year. Although Shō-ichi had hoped they would marry as soon as he returned, he promised he would wait for Haruko to get well, "even if it takes two years," and he visited her every day. When they were finally married in 1956, he was twenty-seven years old and she was twenty-four.

They were married in a simple ceremony in the grounds of the nearby Shintō shrine, and after their four-day honeymoon trip they settled in the new house that Shō-ichi had built across the road from his parents' home. It was a small, two-storied house with only one room on each floor, but Haruko was grateful for the privacy it afforded. "I was always on the alert with my mother-in-law, but when my husband and I went upstairs and were left alone, I felt relieved. I consider myself really lucky to have had that second floor of the other house, especially when I compare myself with those women who sleep with their husband while their mother-in-law lies in the next room, separated only by sliding doors."

For the first ten years of their married life, the couple lived here with their two children but took their meals in the main house with Shō-ichi's mother and siblings. There was only one toilet, in the main house, and the whole family bathed in Bessho's communal bath house, a cause of great distress for Haruko. "If young brides tend to become the center of villagers' curiosity when they are dressed, they are particularly exposed to the gaze of others when they are stark naked. Although some couples went together for their bath, I had been accustomed to bathing in my family's own bath, and I always went with my mother-in-law or took baths at the home of neighbors or relatives."

From the earliest days of her marriage, Haruko worked on her husband's family farm. In the second year, she unintentionally became pregnant, but suffered a miscarriage caused, according to the doctor, by the vibration against her stomach of the gun whose blank cartridges she fired at sparrows in the paddies to scare them away from rice seeds. Half a year later, she became pregnant again. By this time, Shō-ichi, who had begun to take an active part in local politics, was a member of the town assembly, and his mother, suffering from a painful hip condition, could do little work. Haruko became the family's main farm worker. With her legs swollen and her stomach bulging, she continued to work bent over in the wet rice paddies from dawn to dusk throughout the summer weeding season. After Yōko was born, Shō-ichi's mother baby-sat while Haruko continued farming.

Haruko regretted not having had more time to raise her children; "they raised themselves," she said. Unlike women who could stay at home and did not have to farm, Haruko could barely feed and clothe her children, much less help them with their homework or take them anywhere. When Yōko was a baby, Obāsan cared for her during the day, while Haruko worked in the fields. Haruko nursed the baby when she came home to eat lunch. Only on rainy days could she rest and enjoy caring for the baby at her leisure. During the planting and harvesting seasons, when all available labor, including Shō-ichi's still-ailing mother, was required to work in the paddies, Haruko brought Yōko to the fields in a baby carriage and burned straw to keep her warm. In winter she could work with the baby strapped to her back, but in summer it was difficult to bring the baby to the fields at all: if she rode on Haruko's back while Haruko was spraying DDT, she would get sick and throw up; but if she were set down on the ground (since a restless child could not be left all alone in the baby carriage), she would be bitten by bugs. Once, in desperation, Haruko left the infant sleeping alone in the house. She returned to find Yōko had crawled to the paper sliding doors, where she sat tearing at them and crying.

Yōko was a strong-willed child, and to discipline her Haruko tried the traditional Japanese childrearing practices that her mother had used on her: if scolding and spanking proved ineffective, she locked her in the storage shed. Yōko would cry until Obāsan took pity on her and let her out. Once she threw down the dishes stored in the shed. When she was five years old, Yōko deliberately threw out her mother's face powder and on another occasion she broke Haruko's jar of face cream. Haruko responded to such mischief by tying Yōko's hands to a pillar. She also tried moxibustion—igniting on her skin a preparation of powdered leaves in the shape of a small cone—but Yōko was too wily and slipped away.

By the time Hisashi was born, three years after Yōko in 1962, Haruko and Shō-ichi were busier than ever. To supplement their meager farm income, Shō-ichi took out a loan from the Agricultural Cooperative to build a pigsty. Unlike seasonal farm work, the pig business involved them in a daily round of chores throughout the year. It yielded only small profits, however, since the price of pork in those years was low. Shō-ichi was also busy with a variety of public activities. He continued to be a member of the town assembly, on which he served for twelve successive years, and, in addition, he directed a training program that sent young farmers to the United States. During most of her childbearing years, therefore, Haruko remained the family's major farm worker.

During the two-week rice-transplanting season in late May, Haruko's routine never varied. Rising at three in the morning so as not to fall behind in the day's work, she would slip quietly out of the house and walk to the seedbeds, where she picked about a hundred seedlings and tied them together. Then she would walk home again to make breakfast for herself and the children before taking them to a nursery or to the home of an older woman who baby-sat. Returning to the paddies, she would plant seedlings until seven or eight o'clock at night, then walk to the pigsty and feed the pigs in pitch darkness. Since she was too busy to breastfeed Hisashi, she raised him on milk from the family goat. She made the children's clothing herself, knitting sweaters with wool received as gifts when the children were born. She washed their diapers in the stream behind the house.

Almost two decades later, Haruko was still angry about those early years of her marriage. "I envied the wives of the salaried men," Haruko recounted. "Their chores consisted of merely cooking and washing. For farmers' wives, cooking, washing, and caring for children did not count as work. In the morning, my husband and I always worked in the paddies together. If I was late coming out to the field after my housework, he would ask me, 'What were you doing there?' Other women get married; I went as a daughter-in-law. I had not only a husband, but his mother, his brothers, his sisters. Other women can come and go as they please, free to do as they please."

While Haruko's mother-in-law remained the central woman in the household, she continued to do most of the cooking and to manage the household budget, receiving an allowance from Shō-ichi. Whenever Haruko needed money, she had to ask her mother-in-law. "My mother-in-law was not a difficult person to please," she recalled, "but she was calm and a slow mover. Whereas I tend to speak up, she hardly expresses her opinions and feelings. We are not the best companions."

Haruko's situation had been much the same as that of other farm women of her generation married to first sons. Nowadays, Haruko felt, the life of a young farm woman was altogether easier. Some young wives did not even farm. When they complained about their mothers-in-law, Haruko could only wonder at their failure to appreciate the advantages they enjoyed over her own generation. Washing machines, indoor running water, farm equipment—all these material improvements had lightened the housewife's labors. But more importantly, younger farm wives kept their earnings from outside jobs and also received their husband's wages. Today's young couples, less dependent on farming and on their parents for an income, were gaining independence at an earlier age.

Haruko's only source of comfort and advice during the difficult years of her early married life was her own family. In her first three years of marrige, before the birth of her first child, she returned home for two days every month. Her grandmother fixed her favorite foods, let her sleep late, and listened to her complaints. She could not talk so freely with her neighbors in Bessho for fear the gossip would get back to her mother-in-law. Her grandmother, however, could be trusted to listen sympathetically and to give good counsel. On one occasion, hearing that Shō-ichi had shouted impatiently at his wife to "go home," Haruko's grandmother had said jokingly, "Tell your husband that we'll take you back if he can return you the way you were before he married you."

Female relatives—especially grandmothers, mothers, and sisters—lent both emotional and material support to Haruko and other young farm women of her generation. They also offered a temporary escape from the often harsh and demanding world of the young bride's new home. Haruko's mother usually slipped her some spending money and nodded sympathetically as Haruko, at the end of a visit, invariably cried, "I don't want to go back there."

Haruko had come as a stranger to her husband's family and hamlet. If she was an outsider, he was completely familiar with his surroundings. Five of the families in Bessho were related to him by marriage or blood. His roots in Bessho went back several centuries, and the names of his recent ancestors were preserved on tablets on a black lacquer altar in the family's main house, where Shō-ichi's mother made daily food offerings. One day it would be Haruko's responsibility to leave food offerings there.

Bessho breathed the history of the Utsunomiya family. Shō-ichi's great-grandfather had been a Shintō priest. People in the hamlet still remembered his grandfather and his father. Indeed, Shō-ichi himself vividly recalled watching his father build the house they now occupied: it was a larger version of his grandfather's house, rebuilt on the same site, and to celebrate its completion, his father had carried him on his back to the roof and tossed down ceremonial rice cakes.

Shō-ichi knew everyone in the hamlet and the surrounding area. He knew the customs and festival traditions of Bessho, for many of these were passed on by older boys to younger ones in the hamlet. He remembered the words to the song sung by young boys on November 5, Wild Boar's Day, when they go from house to house pounding the earth with rocks—in imitation of the way house foundations are dug—and asking for token gifts of money. He knew the chants sung to the gods during a drought. Shō-ichi belonged to Bessho in a way that Haruko perhaps never could.

If the women in her own family could sympathize with the young wife's complaints, it was because they too had undergone their own painful trials. Haruko's paternal grandfather had squandered part of the family's holdings on geisha and mistresses. The debts he left behind when he died required selling off some of the family's land. His widow, who had never farmed, was forced to work in the rice paddies, and she gave up two of her sons for adoption by other farm families because she could not afford to feed them.

Haruko remembered her grandmother as a source of inspiration to all who knew her: "Grandmother always had a smile on her face. She was kind to others and she was very gentle. She was skillful in sewing, cooking, farming—there was practically nothing she could not do. Neighbors always came to consult with her about local customs. She was always kind enough to answer them. And no matter how hard life was to her, she never complained. She looked on things positively and thought only of the prosperity of the family. In this sense she was a typical Japanese woman."

Yet even this saintly woman dominated her own daughter-in-law, Haruko's mother. "Mother's position in the family, serving under such a fine woman as Grandmother," Haruko recalled, "was understandably weak. Mother's parents were born in a fishing village. They died young, and Mother was raised as an adopted daughter in the home of her uncle. She was about eighteen or nineteen years old when the marriage between her and Father was arranged. Like all young brides, Mother existed to serve Grandmother. Grandmother had the right of decision on all matters.

"When I think of Mother's life, I feel pity for her. There were occasions when even we, her children, sided with Grandmother instead of with her. Even after my brother's marriage, she did not acquire a greater voice in family decision-making, as women usually do after receiving a daughter-in-law. Instead, she continued to be caught between Grandmother and Father. Instead of taking over as mistress of the household, she remained subservient to Grandmother, like a dutiful daughter-in-law, until Grandmother passed away in her eighty-fourth year. By then Mother was already sixty-three. Although she survived the Second World War and the chaos after the war, her suffering and sadness are etched on her very skin."

Haruko remembered her father as a tyrant, a "typical Japanese man" who in moments of anger struck her mother. Embittered by his own father's early death and the economic hardships that afflicted the family afterward, he never forgot his disappointment at having to leave school after only six years of education in order to tend the farm. In 1941 he was drafted into the army. He was captured by the Russians, and he was detained after the war to do forced labor in Siberia. By the time he was repatriated, in 1947, he was a stranger to his children. Upon her father's return, Haruko, who was already fifteen years old, was able to enter senior high school, but after she graduated, he would not support her pleas for further education to enable her to become a schoolteacher. Her dislike of him, rooted in his treatment of her mother, was intensified by his insistence that she help with the farming. "If he had allowed me to do what I wanted, my life would have been quite different."

After conceiving her first child, Haruko felt more settled in Bessho and her visits to her family grew less frequent. "Besides," she recalled, "with a child, I had no other recourse." She paid visits only on New Year's Day, on Obon (a summertime memorial celebration of one's ancestors), and during autumn harvest-festivals. Occasionally she also returned home to attend memorial services for ancestors on her natal family's side.

In times of trouble or illness, however, she continued to rely on her kinfolk for rest and consolation. Once, when Shō-ichi flew into a rage over a kimono she had bought with money she had earned by herself, Haruko grabbed her young daughter and fled to her sister's house in an adjoining hamlet. After crying bitterly for several hours, she returned to her husband's home that evening.

Perhaps the unhappiest years of Haruko's married life were the six years in which she struggled to overcome asthma. In 1964, already weakened by recurrent attacks of bronchitis, she had nevertheless continued to exhaust herself by working in a nearby knitting factory while also tending the pigs, caring for the children, and looking after the farm; and soon the bronchitis developed into asthma. Unable to exert herself, she awoke on some mornings feeling that she was suffocating, and had to be taken to town for injections to aid her breathing. Over the years, she tried a number of cures, including acupuncture. Even a visit to her parents' home to recuperate proved unsuccessful. Finally, in 1970, she tried a drastic treatment that consisted essentially of drinking only water and an expensive medicine for three weeks in order to alter her body's physiology. She continued cooking for the rest of the family but forced herself to fast. At the end of twenty days her health improved, and since then her asthma attacks, though recurrent, have been much less frequent and severe.

Before she reached forty years of age, Haruko had several close brushes with death, and her survival made her believe she was "predestined to have a long life-span." When she was six, she fell into the pond behind her parents' house. An aunt pulled her out just in time.

In the sixth grade, during the war years, she contracted diphtheria and almost died of the high fever. Her mother managed to pay for her treatment by exchanging rice for medicine. At the age of thirty-one Haruko had a third brush with death while pedaling home from town, where she had taken Yōko to see the doctor. She was eight months pregnant with Hisashi at the time. At a railroad crossing, a train suddenly loomed almost on top of her. With one child on her back and another in her belly, she could not react in time and remained immobilized on the tracks. The train stopped, barely a foot away from her.

Shō-ichi too had had a narrow escape from death. In the final months of the war, when he was fifteen years old, he enlisted in naval training school. The school's strict program stressed competitiveness, and the boys regularly performed their chores and exercise drills in teams. The losers were flogged on the buttocks with paddles. "Everyone had scarred seats," Shō-ichi said, and some thirty years later he still remembered the terrible pain of each blow.

One day a single American plane flew over the field where the boys were training and a soldier at the door of the plane began firing down on them. One boy in an open truck was hit in the head and died in front of Shō-ichi's eyes. Shō-ichi ran down the road and dived into a ditch, covering his head with his arms. The plane disappeared into the distance.

One month later, in August 1945, the emperor addressed the country over the radio to announce Japan's surrender. Shō-ichi, like the other boys at his school, feared for his own safety at the hands of the victors. Everyone assumed the occupation army would castrate the Japanese men and send them to the United States as slaves. Women in the prefecture, fearing they would be raped, blackened their faces and dressed in tattered clothes to appear as ugly as possible. But the Americans behaved well, Shō-ichi said, and the United States became a source of inspiration for him as he sought modern farming techniques.

After the war, Shō-ichi finished high school and enrolled in a horticultural college outside Tokyo. He enjoyed his classes and dormitory life, shared with mischievous friends who slipped into farmers' fields at night and stole potatoes to fry for midnight snacks. During the busy farm season, he returned home to help his family. One day he and his father had an argument in the paddies over how to do the work, and Shō-ichi stormed off in anger. Three days later, his father suffered a heart attack and died in the paddies. Shō-ichi had regretted his harsh words ever since.

His father's death left Shō-ichi in full charge of the family. He left college to return to the farm, later completing his degree through correspondence courses. Shō-ichi inherited two acres of land and the family's house, which his father had built over twenty years earlier. Until the end of the war, the family had owned only one and three-quarter acres and had rented another one-quarter acre. Shō-ichi remembered watching his father unload rice sacks from a truck and put them in the landlord's storehouse as rent. Land reforms carried out during the American Occupation enabled Shō-ichi's father to purchase the quarter-acre at a low price, but even so the family's scattered holdings were slightly less than the national average for farmers and were barely enough to support them. With hard work and good luck Haruko and Shō-ichi managed to add another one and one-half acres to their landholdings, bringing the total to three and one-half acres of paddy land. They grew all their own rice and vegetables, with enough surplus to give to relatives and friends in exchange for eggs and tangerines, and Shō-ichi, encouraged by the profit they began to show in their pig business, laid plans to go into partnership with five other men, investing in a business that owned over one thousand pigs.

By the time Haruko and Shō-ichi celebrated their tenth wedding anniversary, in 1966, their living arrangements had also improved, since all of Shō-ichi's brothers and sisters were now married and living elsewhere. Shō-ichi's youngest brother had married several months earlier and had gone to live with his bride's parents as an adopted son-in-law, or *yōshi*, an arrangement that had made his own family, rather than the bride's, responsible for organizing the wedding. The wedding was therefore held in the Utsunomiyas' house, and Shō-ichi used the occasion as an excuse for remodeling the kitchen. At a cost of five hundred fifty dollars, the family installed modern appliances that made cooking easier for the women in the household. Shortly after the wedding of her last child, Obāsan, nearing sixty years of age, retired to the small house across the road, leaving the main house to Shō-ichi, Haruko, and their children. As Japanese farmers say, she "passed the rice scoop" to Haruko, relinquishing her control over domestic matters and allowing Haruko to become the ruling female member of the household, responsible for cooking the meals, representing the family at women's functions, and making consumer decisions. Obāsan gradually receded to the background of family life and Haruko emerged as the central woman of the house. Neighbors, tradesmen, and guests no longer referred to her as *oyome-san*, daughter-in-law, but as *okusan*, the missus or wife.

Having reached a plateau of sorts, in 1971 Haruko and Shō-ichi decided to celebrate their fifteenth wedding anniversary with a trip to Tokyo. Their vacation coincided with a special ceremony at the Imperial Hotel commemorating the twentieth anniversary of the first overseas training program for farmers. Shō-ichi had traveled to the United States under the auspices of this program and had helped train later groups, so this double celebration was a milestone in his life. For Haruko, the trip represented her first visit to the nation's capital and the first time since her honeymoon that she and her husband had been away together. Their one-week stay in a hotel, with neither farming nor housework to do, was the happiest time in her life.

After fifteen years of marriage, the couple's lives had grown a little easier. It was true that, measured in terms of middle-class American standards, they still lived a spartan existence. Their house, like other Japanese-style houses, required few pieces of furniture and lacked central heating. Yet they owned a washing machine, a small car, a pick-up truck, and a motor scooter. Medical treatment was available for only a small fee at the local clinic; and as soon as she reached sixty-five years of age, Obāsan became eligible for free medical treatment and hospitalization as well as a small monthly social security check.

Over the years, Haruko and Shō-ichi had grown more comfortable with each other too, comfortable enough to air their conflicts openly. "It takes at least that long to work out all the differences between a married couple through a lot of arguing and making up," Shō-ichi said. "In your twenties you feel passion," he philosophized, echoing sentiments voiced by others in the countryside. "In your thirties you work toward cooperative effort with your spouse. In your forties you learn forbearance. In your fifties you are finally resigned to each other. And in your sixties you feel *kansha*, gratitude, which is the expression of love."

When I first met Haruko and Shō-ichi, they were in the eighteenth year of their marriage and the fourth decade of their lives, still learning the important Japanese trait of forbearance. For in a number of ways Haruko and Shō-ichi were temperamentally incompatible, and they were also driven into conflict by the different social roles they were expected to play.

Haruko was, in her husband's words, "noisy." She was indeed hyperactive, gabby, and intrusive. When she was feeling well, her physical and mental energy was boundless. But she was also perceptive. For someone who rarely left the confines of her hamlet and almost never had time to read, she demonstrated remarkable empathy and intuitive understanding for circumstances and relationships that were foreign to her. She could immediately grasp my account of academic politics in the United States or unravel the tangled web of emotions of a couple seeking a divorce. She was expert in analyzing human psychology, and she had a comic genius for imitating facial expressions and pinpointing the character traits that made a person unique. Her husband's insights were expressed more subtly, without words and without gestures—one simply sensed that he understood.

Haruko's lively mind, curiosity, and unflagging attention to the details of family life overwhelmed and at times irritated other members of the family. What frequently triggered her husband's annoyance was her nonstop flow of words about matters he found trivial, such as women's fashions. "Too much talk," he would say, softly, in broken English. "Too much talk."

In contrast, Shō-ichi was in his wife's eyes easygoing, slow-paced, devil-may-care. If she always had tasks she wanted him to perform, he always wanted her to settle down and be quiet. When she pushed him to do household chores, he would reply, "The house is for resting and relaxing." Housework, including repairs, was woman's work. Once there was an electrical short in the house and all the lights suddenly went out. The children began arguing with Obāsan whether the outage had hit other houses as well, and Haruko searched the house for a flashlight. We all went out to find the fusebox. In the midst of the confusion we heard Shō-ichi, sitting in the bath in the dark, singing.

"I hate to rush around *gacha-gacha*," Shō-ichi explained later, the onomatopoetic word capturing the unsettling sound of rattling or clanging. Haruko took a different view: "I work and he lounges all day," she said. "He tells me to stop fussing in the kitchen, to 'quit rattling around in there,' but when I finally finish my chores and sit down to watch television with him, he asks me to massage his back."

Calm and soft-spoken, Shō-ichi made a perfect foil for his highly strung, strong-willed wife; but at times their opposite personalities clashed explosively. Haruko's nagging, in the distinctive whining, singsong voice that Japanese women sometimes use, occasionally drove Shō-ichi, for all his gentleness, to lose his temper and strike her. In the early years of their marriage, it was not unusual for him to slap her face or shove her forehead with the palm of his hand. After she started learning Japanese calligraphy and *haiku* poetry-writing, Haruko herself "began to develop some sense of composure," and when Shō-ichi joined the *haiku* society too, the couple found that they were having fewer arguments. Even as they entered middle age, however, Shō-ichi still struck Haruko occasionally.

As long as I was living with the family, Haruko said, he never raised his hand against her. Shortly after I returned home, however, she wrote: "Nothing has changed much with our family since you left, except when we get too rushed, we fight. The other day, my husband hit me. I cried with mortification. We are not as relaxed now as we were in the winter, when you were here. Every day, as soon as it is light out, we go to the paddies to work. Even in bed we are like strangers. We are even tired of each other."

One long-standing source of tension between Haruko and Shō-ichi was too serious to be settled by angry words or by blows. Their continuous struggle centered on Shō-ichi's involvement in community and political activities, which occupied much of his time and left Haruko alone to handle household and farm tasks.

From his earliest years with Haruko, Shō-ichi was forever championing one cause or another that would benefit the people of Bessho and surrounding hamlets. He worked for twelve years on the town assembly. He served as head of the local PTA. He continued his activities in the overseas training program for farmers. He was also a member of the Japan Socialist party.

Shō-ichi's mind and energies were occupied with matters outside the home, in the public realm of meetings and business decisions, of agrarian reform and political office. He preferred to keep the two realms—household and society—separate and distinct, leaving the first in the keeping of his wife. The trouble was that Haruko's own realm of responsibilities involved more than housework. She was also mother, farmer, and occasional wage-earner, and every time Shō-ichi committed himself to a cause, she had to pick up the slack. A case in point was Shō-ichi's leadership in the mechanization of farming in Bessho, a project that represented a decisive change in the lives of everyone in the farm community.

5
Men, Money, and Machinery

HEAVY FARM MACHINERY was introduced in the rice paddies around Bessho in October 1974, and Shō-ichi, who had initiated the project, was eager to give me a guided tour of the autumn harvest. As we watched, four men operated a combine that rode up and down the closely planted rows of rice, cutting the stalks and removing and bagging the rice, all in one operation. Four of these combines, Shō-ichi explained, would replace the labor of all thirty-nine farming households in Bessho, and of the households in four other participating hamlets as well.

Shō-ichi was enormously proud of the new equipment. Mechanized rice-farming in Bessho was the culmination of a twenty-year-old dream. In 1955, when he was twenty-five, he was chosen to join one of the first farm study-groups to go to the United States. Crossing the great wheat and potato fields of the Midwest, he had been awed by the huge scale of farming in the United States and by the use of machinery in place of human labor to plant and harvest crops. In those days, farming in Bessho was still done by traditional means— the labor of men, women, and children of all ages, and oxen. Electricity, indoor running water, and automobiles simply did not exist in Bessho. Farmers drew water in buckets from a well and their sole means of transportation from house to field was the bicycle. The use of machinery in the United States, and the vastness of individual farmholdings there, left an indelible impression on Shō-ichi. Now, almost twenty years later, he was master-minding agricultural reforms that promised to produce similar farming conditions on a smaller scale in his own community.

A major obstacle to the mechanization of farming in Japan had always been the lack of capital to pay for machines; another was the smallness and fragmentation of the landholdings. For hundreds of years the average landholding in Japan has been two and one-half acres, a figure that includes not only the family's rice-paddy and vegetable land, but their house and storage shed. A family's farmland, moreover, was scattered in various parts of the hamlet, divided up into plots of land so small that each resembled the front lawn or the vegetable garden of an American suburban dweller. "My father's land was scattered here and there over several acres," Shō-ichi remarked. "We spent a lot of time walking from one paddy to another."

It was unreasonable to expect any one family to invest in costly and large equipment to work such minuscule pieces of land: clearly, the introduction of modern farm equipment must be preceded by a reorganization of the landholdings. After Shō-ichi returned from his one-year stay in the United States, he began to formulate a plan to unite five of the hamlets ringing the periphery of the rice plain. He proposed to redistribute the land so that each farmer's paddies formed a single, self-contained unit. His plan involved relocating the individual owner's land, but not diminishing the total size of the holding. "A man can still say, 'This is my land,' " Shō-ichi told me.

He continued by pointing out the difference between the land lying to the south of us, where the bulldozer had already visited, and the land lying to the north of us. To the south of the narrow dirt path on which we were standing, I saw a miniature Midwest America: checkerboard squares. To the north, I saw a jigsaw puzzle of paddies, some not more than nine feet long, some triangular, some long and narrow. I secretly preferred the traditional patterns for their diverse shapes and their small, human scale, but Shō-ichi found his mini-Midwest beautiful, and I knew he meant tidy, rational, organized, and efficient. It was the difference between something that had grown naturally and something that had been planned, between asymmetry and balance, between variety and order.

Walking back to the house, we passed the hamlet social hall and

Shō-ichi took me inside to show me the map he had drawn with the help of the Unomachi Town Hall to rearrange the land. It was torn and tattered. "I've folded and unfolded it so many times," he said, smiling. "In the beginning," he said, "people were afraid to invest their money in machines. Also, they wanted to continue ploughing their own fields by themselves. But their work was inefficient. It used to take one man an entire day to cut a quarter-acre of rice. With machines, it takes four operators one day to cut and thresh four acres. Twenty years ago, we worked from four-thirty in the morning till seven at night for two weeks at harvest time just cutting rice."

The new machines would not produce more rice, Shō-ichi added, nor would they yield greater profits. Widening the fields might even make the growing surface smaller, because wider roads would be built around the periphery of the rice plain; in fact, the Utsunomiya house would have to be moved back off the road onto part of the paddy fields behind it. "What new machinery will do is make farming less physically demanding and release farmers to do other things. The money we earn in pig businesses, for example, or in construction work or tobacco growing, will replace the savings we spent to purchase the machines. Tobacco alone, grown after the rice paddies are harvested, can yield three times the profit rice does. A couple farming a little over an acre of tobacco can earn as much as $3,300 annually. But it takes technical know-how. You have to study. For this reason, farmers have been reluctant to stop growing rice, even though profits from rice are relatively low."

In the past year the program of *kōzō kaizen*, or structural reform in rice farming, had finally gained acceptance. It was increasingly apparent, Shō-ichi explained, that farmers could no longer live by farming alone. The growth of industry had raised the standard of living of the wage earner and the townsman, but it had also raised prices. Farm income could not rise to meet this higher level, because there is a natural limit to agricultural productivity, and also because the government fixes rice prices. A soaring inflation rate that in 1974 reached thirty percent had forced farmers to seek outside sources of income. Of the forty-five households in Bessho, all but six farmed, but half of the male farmers derived their main income from full-time employment in nearby factories or in civil-service or other office jobs in town. Of the remainder, one worked full time as a postman, another as a schoolteacher; and others supplemented their farm incomes by working part time as life-insurance salesmen, carpenters, and construction workers, or by raising chickens or keeping one or two cows, which, in the absence of grazing land, had to be tethered in narrow stalls.

As long as the Japanese economy continued to expand, Shō-ichi went on, farmers could keep up with the inflationary rise in prices by taking on outside jobs. But since these jobs were more readily available in the cities, the population in the countryside had been declining. This was another reason machines were welcome. When there was still a surplus farm population, the incentive for introducing costly machines was minimal. To be sure, Bessho's farmers had used small machinery, such as mechanical threshers, since the 1950's, and in 1971 they began using cutting machines. But heavier equipment, such as the combine, had until recently been considered too big and too costly.

By the 1970's, however, Japanese manufacturers were producing smaller combines, scaled-down versions of American equipment; and government loans and grants to the farmers were making mechanization programs affordable. Thus Shō-ichi's own machine cooperative received a low-interest loan from the Ministry of Agriculture and Forestry to cover seventy percent of the cost of reorganizing the paddy fields and fifty percent of the cost of the combines. The loan was payable over twenty-five years. The remaining costs were covered by an outright grant.

"One final reason I was able to convince farmers in this area to cooperate," Shō-ichi said, "is that this year the government has been talking about abolishing its farm-subsidy program. The Japanese government, like the American government, has been paying farmers not to produce rice, because the rice surplus was depressing farm prices. The subsidy discouraged farmers from investing in farm equipment, since they could make more money simply by not farming at all." Making the farms pay for themselves by traditional methods, and without government subsidy, would have required that many of the farmers somehow contrive to take time away from their other, full-time jobs in order to work in the paddies during the planting and harvesting seasons.

The summer of 1974 saw the realization of the first stage of Shō-ichi's plan to mechanize farming in the Bessho area. Together with officials from the Town Hall, he put the finishing touches to his map. The cost of widening the 280 acres of paddy fields was $1,000 per quarter acre. He hired a local contractor who brought in bulldozers to level the roads and dikes separating one paddy field from another and built new roads around the circumference. Women were hired to remove rocks and boulders and help lay simple bridges spanning irrigation ditches. In early June, for the first time in the area's history farmers from the five hamlets planted the entire rice plain together.

Shō-ichi felt like a general, planning the details and giving orders to the farmers. On the first morning, he recalled, everyone lined up at the Bessho social hall to receive his commands: "You drive the truck, you tie the seedlings." Shō-ichi himself drove a tractor. Children were gathered on the second floor of the hall and supervised by an elderly woman from the hamlet and a younger woman from the Agricultural Cooperative. The Women's Guild supplied snacks of bread, cakes, and milk. After the men had completed the harrowing, one hundred women lined up across the breadth of the paddy fields to transplant the rice seedlings into the flooded paddies. "Women work faster than men," Shō-ichi explained. "Their fingers are more delicate and agile." Haruko could transplant three times as fast as he could; indeed, she was well ahead of all the other women on that proud day.

Within two weeks the entire plain was covered with rice seedlings from one end to the other. When the transplanting was completed, the farmers all drank beer and shouted a toast of "Banzai." Shō-ichi wept.

Organizing the machine cooperative was the crowning achievement of Shō-ichi's life, the realization of his dream of twenty years. In the fall of the same year the four combines, owned jointly by Bessho and the other four hamlets, harvested the rice for the first time. The following summer, mechanized rice-transplanters would per-

The rice plain in 1974. *Top*: The northern part of the plain, showing the traditional arrangement of paddies with their multiplicity of shapes. *Bottom*: The southern part of the plain, showing at the upper left the reorganized, regularly shaped paddies. At the lower right is the hamlet of Bessho.

Above: In June 1974 over one hundred women lined up across the rice plain to transplant the rice seedlings. The following year the work would be done by mechanized rice transplanters. *Right*: Shō-ichi operates a mechanized hand tractor in a potato field. *Below*: Hired laborers harvest rice with one of the new combines in the fall of 1974.

form work that had required the labor of all the women working ten hours a day for two weeks.

Ironically, the new machines were a major source of conflict between Shō-ichi and Haruko. I had been living in their house less than two weeks when they had a mild argument over the cost of the new equipment. Shō-ichi had just returned from a drinking session with some of the men in the machine cooperative. Toward the end of the evening meal he and Haruko began arguing whether to use the family's savings to help buy more machinery, such as a mechanical rice-planter and another combine, or to keep the money in savings and do some of the planting and harvesting by hand, as they had always done it. Although the additional machinery seemed likely to free Haruko from much physical drudgery, she opposed her husband's ambitious plans.

"What if we get sick and can't work?" she asked. "We won't have any money."

"She's tight about money," Shō-ichi said to me, still mellow with drink.

Haruko repeated, "What if we can't work? Why must we sacrifice for everyone else?"

Haruko resented the time her husband spent on the administrative and accounting side of the reforms. He devoted hours of work to keeping careful records that were audited regularly by prefectural and national government accountants. Figuring costs was a tedious chore for him. There was the cost of the community's bulk purchases of fertilizer, for example, to be shared according to each family's land-holdings. There was also the shared cost of paying the machine operators, to be determined, not by the time actually spent in working each family's holdings, but by the time the families themselves would have spent in working the holdings. Then again there was the matter of repaying the farmers who participated in the preparation of the fields. Shō-ichi volunteered his own services as a bookkeeper free of charge, conscientiously poring over the records, which were kept in a little office on the ground floor of the hamlet social hall.

Shō-ichi also spent many hours on the political aspects of the reforms, assuaging doubts, convincing the more timid members of the hamlet, negotiating with government representatives, and promoting rapport among his associates in the enterprise by ironing out differences over a friendly drink. For many years Haruko had shouldered the burden of raising the children, feeding the pigs on the nights when he arrived home late, and sitting alone in the evening waiting for him to return. "There were whole days when he never saw his children," she said, angrily.

Shō-ichi turned to me. "One cannot live without ideals, without a dream."

Haruko snickered, turned her back, and began washing the dishes.

"What led you to organize the machine cooperative?" I asked Shō-ichi.

"One reason is pride. One must have something to live for. And perhaps you could say 'humanism.' Merely to do your own work for yourself—that's meaningless and petty as far as I'm concerned. The Japanese family system encourages people to worry only about their own. Even at an early age, I wanted to go out into society. And I feel obligated to the group that paid my way when I went to study in the United States."

"Did you never think of doing anything besides farming?" I asked.

"When I was younger, I hoped to be a high school teacher," Shō-ichi replied. "But I went to talk with the local high school teacher and somehow lost my interest. I was born into a farm family. I like farming. I feel free. I'm my own boss. And I like working with nature. It's a challenge."

Shō-ichi meant, of course, progressive farming, with machines. He hoped to be a gentleman farmer. His enthusiasm for modern methods seemed nevertheless to be tinged with some regret for the demise of the old style of farming, and in particular for the passing of the old spirit of communality he associated with it. It was true that the recent modernization efforts had aroused a certain spirit of cooperation, indeed had demanded it, but somehow it was not the same as the feeling you got from laboring together in the paddies.

Almost wistfully, Shō-ichi recalled that in the old days the hamlet was like a large family. If the monsoon season was late in arriving, everybody prayed together for the precious rains needed to irrigate

the paddies. They also took turns maintaining a watch over the irrigation ponds, to prevent "robbers" from nearby hamlets from
trying to divert river water to their own fields. If someone in the hamlet was dying, they gathered together to chant sutras for hours at a
time: older men taught the chants to the young people. And, of
course, they organized in groups to share farm equipment, to rebuild
a neighbor's house if it burned down, to cut trees in the communally
owned woods beyond the hamlet. Groups of four or five households
close to each other formed *kumi* or mutual work teams, and the
women in these teams for generations catered each other's weddings
and funerals. This traditional spirit of communality was further
strengthened every autumn with a festival in which the entire hamlet
participated, celebrating the joy of the harvest.

"But praying for the sick is different from sharing economic costs,"
Shō-ichi said. The old communal spirit was different from the spirit
of cooperation needed for survival in today's capitalist society. "We
must break away from the old style of farming in tiny, privately
owned paddies and band together to gain economic strength."

If Haruko and Shō-ichi, in different ways, privately voiced concern
over the new course on which they had embarked, misgivings and
doubts were openly expressed by other members of the community.
They claimed, for example, that their rice had tasted better in previous years, when their paddies had been located one-quarter mile
away from their newly assigned land. In spite of such complaints,
Shō-ichi remained calm and conciliatory, even when a drunken
farmer burst in upon our dinner hour to grumble.

To some farmers in the hamlet, Shō-ichi's plans for modernization
seemed to call for the right thing too late. Farmers throughout Japan
voice the fear that their farms will not have an *ato-tsugi*, literally a
"follow-after"—a successor. The lure of city life threatens the countryside, where children, no longer needed to work on the farms,
watch Jack Nicklaus play golf on television or listen for hours on end
to matinee idols on the radio.

Thanks to their education, the boys will want to become "salaried
men" when they grow up, and the girls will want to marry salaried
men. Indeed, the dearth of women willing to marry farmers has ne-

cessitated the establishment of Bridal Banks, often under the auspices of the Agricultural Cooperatives, which help arrange marriages for farm heirs. Young women do not want to marry farmers, they say, because farming is "dirty" or because they are unwilling to endure the physical demands and economic insecurity of the farmer's life. Married to a city wage-earner, they could live apart from their in-laws, stay at home during the day to practice the housewifely skills of cooking and sewing, and in general pursue the bourgeois ideal so glamorously portrayed in television commercials and magazines.

A contradiction thus haunts present-day Japanese farmers. Eager to give their children a good education in order to improve their material way of life, they are raising young people inexperienced in farming and prejudiced against it. Parents who sacrifice for their children's future are in effect sacrificing their own futures, cutting themselves off from the prospect of preserving the family property. Moreover, they are consigning themselves to a lonely old age, without their son and daughter-in-law to live with them on the farm and care for them, as generations of elder sons have done.

To be sure, older people can always hire laborers to work their land; and they can rent their land or even sell it. But as Shō-ichi said, "If a farmer cannot work his own land by himself, then farming loses its meaning."

The fate of many farm families is thus threatened by their bright, ambitious sons and daughters. Indeed, the wealthier the community, the greater the likelihood that its population of young people will decline, as it finances its children's education as lawyers, teachers, or company executives. A hamlet near Bessho which for generations had been the most prosperous of the six hamlets that ring the rice plain was inhabited in the 1970's mainly by old people: only four men under the age of forty engaged in farming during the planting and harvesting season.

Facing up to these realities, Shō-ichi held fast to his dream of reshaping the economy and even the life-style of the traditional Japanese peasant-farmer into that of an agribusinessman. By glamorizing farming and making it more profitable, he hoped to reverse the exodus of young men from the land. Farm machinery and motorized vehicles would accomplish the first goal, minimizing the physical drudgery of rice cultivation, and new cash crops, such as tobacco and wheat, would achieve the second.

The achievement of both goals required further training of the farmers, and to this end, Bessho and other communities in Ehime prefecture and throughout Japan were sending their sons to the United States to learn modern farming techniques under the auspices of programs sponsored by the Japanese government. In 1968 Shō-ichi himself had returned to the United States to study farm management at Yuma Western College in Arizona, and among his chief supporters in the hamlet were several young men in their late twenties and early thirties who had recently returned from two years spent in farming communities in Oregon, Nebraska, California, and Arizona. They were learning how to operate tractors and bulldozers, and investing in side-enterprises, such as grape vines.

What struck one about these young men was the extent to which American farm ways had rubbed off on them. Dressed in levis, operating tractors, and letting their young wives stay home rather than work in the fields the way Haruko did, they epitomized the new breed of farmers whom Shō-ichi was trying to train. Like Shō-ichi, they were demonstrating that it might be possible for farmers to earn a living without taking factory jobs, commuting, or living away from home six months out of the year, provided they could rationalize their operations, experiment with new crops, and invest in modern equipment.

6

Haruko's Work

"I LEAD a relatively relaxed life," Haruko told me, kneeling on the floor, folding the laundry, a few days after my arrival in Bessho. "I have a circle of four or five close friends who are, like myself, only housewives. Most other women in this area work outside in factories or stores. I prefer not to work, because I don't need the money that much and would rather have free time. Working women are so busy they don't have time to help their husbands." I gradually discovered that in reality she had very little free time; in fact she had stayed home from work only to help me get settled.

During the first weeks of my stay, the pace of Haruko's daily routine quickened noticeably. It soon became evident that she was more than just "a housewife." Although machinery had freed both women and men from most of the arduous work of rice cultivation, many other farming chores remained, and they usually fell to the women. In addition, once the harvest season was over, Haruko, like most other women in Bessho, sought part-time wage-paying work nearby. Watching her daily activities over several months, I concluded that Haruko was the busiest member of her family.

Yet it was not always easy to ascertain exactly what work Haruko and other farm women performed. For one thing, farm women did not consider their round of household chores to be work, and they viewed vegetable farming as merely an extension of their domestic sphere of activity—a part of cooking. Nor did they define rice cultivation as work. Even though they had labored side by side with men in the paddies, transplanting rice seedlings in late spring or early summer, weeding together with other women during the remainder of the summer, and again working with their menfolk during the harvest in early fall, farm women referred to such labor as "helping my husband." Only wage labor constituted work. Thus to rely on simple questions like, "What work do you do?" was to invite deceptive answers, because even women who farmed almost entirely on their own but were not employed "outside" for pay, might reply, "I do not work; I stay at home."

In addition, women's work included numerous separate, discrete tasks that varied according to the season of the year and the time of day, and that were performed in countless different places inside and outside the house, the shed, and other farm buildings and on various plots of land scattered throughout the hamlet. Every day I had to ask Haruko where she would be working, and even after she told me, "I'll be hoeing in the vegetable field," I often could not find her, because the family farmed several vegetable fields in different places. By the time I did locate her, she might be finished with the hoeing and on to another task, such as separating out the weeds from the edible grasses she had picked the day before.

Equally difficult to study was the diversity of part-time, wage-paying jobs women performed. Their jobs in factories, shops, and offices or as orderlies in hospitals and as day laborers on other farmers' land took them out of the hamlet during the day. To observe such work required trailing after each hamlet woman and gaining entry into half a dozen different work sites. Also, the work was often temporary: small factories hiring only a few women might close down for several months during an economic slump, and women working as agricultural hired hands might be laid off after the harvest was over.

By tagging after Haruko for several months, I was eventually able to compile a list—by no means complete—of her work responsibilities. They fell broadly into three categories: homemaking, farming, and wage earning.

As a homemaker, Haruko had more extensive responsibilities than ever before: not only was she in charge of such traditional domestic work as cooking, cleaning, sewing, and participating in communal functions, but in recent years she had assumed the newer tasks of shopping, paying the bills, and guiding her children's education. Except in matters relating to the children, Shō-ichi, like most Japanese men, removed himself altogether from these domestic concerns.

Haruko's daily round of household chores began at six o'clock, when recorded Westminster chimes, broadcast from the loudspeaker installed on the roof of the hamlet social hall, awakened the farmers of Bessho and set her scurrying around the house. Every morning she prepared a breakfast of *misoshiru* (bean-paste soup enriched with white cubes of bean curd, an egg, and a few garden greens), boiled rice, and green tea. The children, who needed to be coaxed awake, ate toasted white bread. Before sitting down to breakfast at seven o'clock, Haruko placed six cups of green tea as offerings on the Buddhist altar in the bedroom. Whenever she made special food, such as rice balls, she also offered some to *hotoke-sama*, the spirits of the ancestors of Shō-ichi's family.

After sending the children off to school at eight o'clock in a flurry of last-minute searches for clothing and books and hastily delivered instructions, Haruko ran a load of wash in the washing machine and hung it out to dry. She also aired the heavy mattresses and quilts to prevent mildew, a perennial problem in Japan's humid climate. These two tasks were part of her morning routine on every clear day, but regardless of the weather, at five o'clock every single evening, just before starting dinner, she filled the deep bath tub with hot water for the family's bath. Going without the daily bath was unthinkable; and if Haruko was detained, Obāsan or Yōko did this chore in her place. Her routine did not include housecleaning, however. There were neither windows to wash nor furniture to dust, and since shoes were removed at the door, the tatami-covered floor remained clean and required only sweeping. Such cleaning as was necessary was relegated to rainy days, when farmers do not work in the fields.

Lunch was a simply prepared meal of rice, processed or raw fish, and leftovers. For dinner, taken punctually at six o'clock, Haruko again made boiled rice, this time served with numerous side dishes, each on its own little plate, such as raw tuna or mackerel, boiled octopus, sliced vinegared cucumbers, noodles, seaweed, or spinach sprinkled with sesame seeds, and green tea. Thanks to Shō-ichi's pig business the family enjoyed more meat than other farm families, and occasionally they also ate small cubes of fried chicken bought at the Agricultural Cooperative supermarket in Unomachi.

As the woman of the house, Haruko also had several traditional community obligations that were impossible to shirk. Custom demands that all the women in a *kumi* (a grouping of several neighboring households) help prepare food for receptions following the funerals or weddings of member families. Furthermore, each household sends one woman to attend regular meetings of the Women's Guild of the Agricultural Cooperative Association. Haruko and other Bessho farm wives took turns serving in administrative capacities within the guild. They also participated in the cooking classes sponsored by the guild, as well as in meetings of the Parent-Teacher Association.

In addition to being a homemaker, Haruko was the family's chief farm worker. She grew the fruits and vegetables consumed by the household almost entirely on her own: carrots, peppers, Chinese cabbage, spinach, strawberries, broccoli, corn, onions, and a small scallion called *nira*. In the summertime, after the rice crop was planted, she prepared year-long supplies of staple food items such as pickled vegetables and bean paste for *misoshiru*, and she further supplemented the family diet with wild grasses picked in the hills surrounding the rice plain or along the road. Once, when Haruko was not feeling well, Shō-ichi offered to plant the onions, but she had to tell him what to do.

Since the money for modernizing agriculture had been diverted primarily to the rice paddies, vegetables were still grown in tiny, scattered fields. Haruko's garden was actually four different plots of land: a vegetable patch in front of the house, another one across the road from the house, a cabbage patch down the road toward town, and a potato field about a half mile away in the opposite direction. While the men were learning to use the new rice-transplanting machines and the combines, Haruko worked with an old iron grubbing fork and a scythe. To enrich the soil, she relied on organic materials: chicken manure for fertilizer, and chicken feathers and rice husks for mulch. To irrigate a nearby vegetable field, she drew water from a spigot in front of the goldfish pond and carried it in a watering can.

Haruko did not always farm alone. For one week in autumn, for example, she worked with Obāsan and Shō-ichi harvesting potatoes, which were grown on a quarter-acre plot and fed to the pigs. (Farmers who ate mainly potatoes during the war do not care for them now, though their children have developed a taste for them.) The three worked silently in the fields from ten o'clock in the morning until five at night, stopping only for one hour at noon, when a siren announced the lunch break, and again at three o'clock, when they took a snack of green tea, tangerines, and a sweet cake. The women's work consisted of cutting the potato vines with a scythe, arranging them in piles, and tying them together. Then they put the potatoes in sacks for Shō-ichi to load onto his truck. Shō-ichi also operated a small, motor-driven plow that turned over the soil after the potatoes were harvested. Neighbors carted away the vines and fed them to their cows.

Haruko also worked with her mother-in-law and husband on a neighborhood team husking rice. The group, which included Obāsan's sister and the sister's husband, son, and daughter-in-law, together with two neighbors, had collectively purchased a wooden husking machine in the early 1960's. It was run by a generator. Before purchasing the husker, they had paid a husking company to do the job for them, and before that, when Obāsan came to Bessho as a bride, a hand-operated device had been used to turn the rice around for hours at a time. The fall of 1974 was the last time the husking group would work together; beginning with the next harvest, all the rice would be husked mechanically in a large machine operated by the Agricultural Cooperative.

Members of the husking group took turns husking rice at each other's houses, and the host family was expected to provide refreshments. On the morning when it was their turn to use the machine, Obāsan and Haruko were up early getting the house in order and preparing the food. While Obāsan raked a gravel area in front of the house, where the gangling wooden contraption would be set up, Haruko turned on the rice steamer, made a swipe at the cobweb strung from the overhead lampshade in the living room to the side wall, climbed the persimmon tree for some fruit, leaped on her scooter for a quick errand to town, and, upon returning, set out the straw baskets used to carry the family's rice kernels from the storage shed to the husker. Shō-ichi telephoned to town for an order of beer.

Once the work team assembled (all but one worker arrived at exactly eight o'clock), the women and the men worked separately on each side of the husker. There was no need to delineate chores or to explain how the work would be done: everyone knew exactly what to do. The women filled the straw baskets with rice, hauled them to the machine, and poured in the rice, while the men weighed the husked rice as it flowed out of the machine, recorded the amount, and sacked and hauled the rice back to the storage shed.

Two hours later, the work was done and a mid-morning feast was served. Mats were spread out between the machine and the side of the road. The workers gathered in a circle, the women on one side, kneeling, and the men on the other, sitting cross-legged. An abundance of food was pressed on the guests, who ritually refused once or twice before accepting rice cakes, raw fish, assorted vegetables, hard-boiled eggs, fruit, tea, beer, and *sake*. Haruko peeled persimmons, cut them into four slices each, and handed them around. Sitting on dust and gravel by the side of the road, after two hours of labor, it was nevertheless possible at that moment to feel like royalty being wined and dined, filling one's belly, laughing and joking, indulged by the host and hostess, whose turn to be served would come the following day, when the wooden husker would be wheeled down the road to work at another house.

One of Haruko's principal farm chores was feeding the pigs, which were housed in a wooden structure several hundred yards behind the house. More than half of the Utsunomiyas' annual income came from the pig business. Twice a day, once in the morning and once at night, the couple fed the ninety pigs and cleaned the pigsty. There were about twelve pens, with seven or eight pigs in each. Haruko poured feed into the trough and mixed water in with it, while her husband cleaned the pens one by one, shoveling out the dung. They worked quickly and in silence. The stench and the flies seemed not to trouble either of them.

"Which of your tasks do you least like?" I asked Haruko one day, emerging from the pigsty to take a deep breath of fresh air. The air inside the sty was suffocating, and the pink, flesh-colored pigs, crowded into their stalls, were loudly squealing for food. Haruko was pouring feed from a tank into a wheelbarrow. Without looking up, she answered, "If you farm, you can't say you hate any work."

Shō-ichi operated a larger pig business in the mountains about twenty minutes' drive from the house. He and five other men raised one thousand pigs and took turns staying overnight to feed the animals, clean the pens, and tend to any emergencies.

Occasionally Haruko went along to help Shō-ichi and the other men at the pig farm. Neither she nor her husband showed any sentimentality toward the animals. A mother pig, too exhausted after giving birth to move into the warmer quarters prepared for her and her piglets, and uncomfortable with a stillborn infant inside her, was first punched and then prodded with a hog catcher that was attached to her snout. Dead piglets from other litters lay in the aisle between the pens. Frightened pigs being weighed for market were kicked in the face, pulled by the ears or tails, or punched on their backs to make them heed. Haruko seemed unperturbed by the din of grunts and squeals, and while some of the men loaded pigs in a basket onto a truck, she calmly swept one of the sties. When the truck drove off, she put down her broom and stood on the pig scale to weigh herself.

An important part of pig farming was mating the pigs. As soon as the male was led into the female's pen, he became aroused, but he could not perform without assistance. Shō-ichi helped guide the penis, and if the pig failed to penetrate, he punched him as a reminder to try again. It took about ten to fifteen minutes to align a pair; copulation itself took only a few seconds. Meanwhile, Haruko stood ready to help, opening the gates to the pen or simply standing on the sidelines cheering and offering advice, like a third-base coach at the world series. "A little higher," she would yell, or "Oh, oh, too bad. OK now, off to the right a bit," alternately laughing at and sympathizing with the efforts of both pig and husband. She shared fully in her husband's work—it was equally her work—and the two performed their tasks like partners.

By early November, Haruko usually looked for part-time, wage-paying jobs. In previous years, she had worked in a small textile factory in Bessho. She had also commuted by bus to Akehama township to pick tangerines as a day laborer, earning four dollars a day (at a time when a tube of lipstick cost five dollars), but since she had returned home from that job too late to prepare the bath and fix dinner, she decided to look for work closer to home. Her options were limited, however.

The local economy offered various small jobs that called for manual dexterity, such as scraping barnacles off oyster shells, wrapping pastry in leaves, or planting tobacco seedlings with chopsticks. This work was often unappealing, however: it usually required either sitting or hunkering for hours at a time, and in such jobs as tobacco planting one was not paid until the crop was harvested and sold.

A few women from Bessho had found office or sales positions in Unomachi, but these positions required special training. When I asked Haruko whether she could get an office job in town, perhaps at the telephone company, where a younger hamlet woman worked, she replied tersely, "I don't have the qualifications." Besides, some of these jobs required a full-time commitment. The best-paying jobs for women, she added, were jobs as schoolteachers, clerks in government offices, shopkeepers, and factory workers. Her own opportunities were confined largely to manual labor.

When day laborers were needed during the reorganization of the rice paddies, Haruko was taken on as a *dokata*, or construction worker (literally, a "mud person"), and she worked on a team with two other women and three men. In most other wage-paying jobs women and men worked apart, at distinct kinds of work, but on the construction teams they worked side by side. The women were paid about $6.65 a day for eight hours' work, and the men were paid about $11.65.* They took one hour for lunch and two additional breaks of one-half hour each.

The female *dokata*'s work was physically demanding: women hauled heavy boulders, climbed down into trenches to lay irrigation

*Money values have been calculated from the fall 1974 exchange rate of 300 yen = U.S. $1.00.

pipes, constructed bridges over irrigation ditches, and shoveled snow from steep mountain slopes. Though they feminized their work outfits with aprons and bonnets, some were embarrassed when I asked them what work they did, and one female *dokata* replied indirectly, "I do the same work as Haruko."

The *dokata*'s work could be hazardous, too, especially for women unaccustomed to it. In early January, after two months on the construction crew, Haruko was hit on the side of the head by a falling rock. Although her employer had distributed helmets to all workers, Haruko did not like to wear hers. By a freak coincidence, her head was hit by another falling rock the very next day; she was wearing only her bonnet. This time she began to suffer fainting spells, dizziness, and headaches that prevented her from riding her motor scooter. X-rays did not reveal any bone damage, but the doctor decided that her "nerves" had been affected and prescribed one month's bed rest and a daily dose of eighteen tablets. She was also instructed not to take baths or wash her hair until she recovered. By the end of the month she was feeling better, though a brain scan now showed some abnormality and she had recurrent attacks of asthma. Daily injections at the hospital helped control the asthma; but whenever she tried to work in the fields, the headaches returned. National health insurance and her employee's insurance covered both the bulk of her medical expenses and her loss of income.

Haruko much preferred farming to construction work, she said. She was not thinking of hazards, however, or of physical demands; it was simply that she favored farming over any kind of wage labor. As a farmer, she could see the results of her endeavors. "The greatest pleasure of farming is the autumn harvest," she commented, and on more than one occasion she spoke of the "joy of producing one's own food," and of her "pride" in being the wife of a farmer. She also liked being able to work alongside her husband. Another advantage of farming was that "the farmer is master of himself; he can do whatever he chooses to do." In contrast, outside labor meant "you are used by others." When Haruko had worked in the Bessho knitting mill, she had always been watching the clock, "driven by time," because wages were determined by the worker's productivity—the number of finished goods she produced. Women stood hour after tedious hour in front of the machines, pushing a bobbin from right to left.

Not all farm women shared Haruko's views. Five women working in the Bessho mill, a one-room operation owned by a man in Yawatahama, said they enjoyed the piecework he sent them to do. "Paddy work is hard labor," said one woman. "This is easy." Another said, "We all live in Bessho. We are like relatives. It's pleasant here. Sometimes we sing songs." They worked their own hours, after the farm season was over. From late November they spent most of their time in the factory; in December, however, the factory abruptly closed down, a victim of market fluctuations caused by the oil scarcity in late 1974.

Women working in larger, more impersonal factories echoed some of Haruko's sentiments about factory work. In *Minori* (Harvest) magazine, published by the Women's Guild of Uwa township, one woman voiced her complaints: "When I first started working, I felt uneasy about leaving the housework and the children, but there was no other way to pick up ready cash. Under today's completely changed work conditions, nerve fatigue, more than physical labor, is what quickly gets to you. You have to learn your work. You have to think about dealing with people you are working with in the organization. You have a lot of different feelings when you go out working. And you think: Aren't you taking money but making plainer meals? Can you really manage the household? Are you really taking care of your children's and your husband's health if you come home tired? By working [outside the home] won't you make your family unhappy?"

Factory work in Higashiuwa county consisted primarily of making blue jeans (called g-pants) and canning and packing *mikan* (Japanese tangerines). Women working in blue-jeans factories could earn between $5.60 and $6.60 a day, depending on their experience and the number of jeans they completed. In one factory in Nomura township, women worked from eight in the morning until five at night, with one hour for lunch. Each woman received a flat wage for working on one part of the pants and a bonus depending on the group's productivity as a whole. In a *mikan*-packing plant operated by the Agricul-

Sample Daily Wages Paid to Female Workers in Higashiuwa County in 1975
(U.S. dollar equivalent)[a]

JOB	WOMEN'S WAGES	MEN'S WAGES
Dokata in Bessho	6.80 + disability insurance	11.90
Jeans factory in Nomura	5.60–6.60 + bonus	
Mikan-packing plant in Unomachi	5.10 + disability insurance + bonus	
Mikan-packing plant in Yawatahama	7.14–8.50	
Piecework at home	1.20	
Silkworm cultivation in Nomura	7.82	
Textile factory in Nomura	5.10–5.80	11.90
Tobacco planting in nursery beds in Bessho[b]	7.82	9.52
Construction work in cities		16.00–20.00 after room and board
Pruning trees in commonly held forest in Bessho	70% of men's wages	
Rice transplanting in Bessho	equal wages with men	
Public works projects in Bessho	equal wages with men if woman is single head of household	

NOTE: A blank entry indicates that the information in question was either unavailable or inapplicable.

[a] Computed from the 1975 rate of 294 yen = U.S. $1.00. Some wages had recently been raised by 300–500 yen.

[b] The women placed tobacco seedlings into containers; the men did the planning, organizing, and record keeping. The women were paid their wages only after the crop was sold.

tural Cooperative in Unomachi, the women earned $5.10 for eight hours of work; in Yawatahama, about thirty minutes away by train, similar work paid between $7.14 and $8.50. Daily wages in the cooperative's plant were supplemented by a bonus, however, and by disability insurance like the *dokata*'s wages, which meant that the workers' real income in effect compared respectably with that of other non-salaried workers in the county (see the accompanying table), and was actually greater than that of a *dokata*, who did not work on rainy days.

Whereas the canning plant's equipment for folding and stapling cartons and sending fruit speeding along the conveyor belts was both modern and efficient, conditions of work were neither: some women knelt on cushions in a dimly lit, unheated building placing fruit into

Women working in a blue-jeans factory.

Haruko (upper left) works on a construction team building a bridge over an irrigation ditch.

Haruko's next-door neighbor, as a temporary worker at a tobacco nursery, transplants seedlings with chopsticks.

Below: Haruko (left) and a member of her husking group carry baskets of rice from the storage shed to the wooden husking machine in front of her house.

cartons, and others stood under a bare electric lightbulb separating out damaged fruit. Factory work was sought after because it paid a wage, but as a contributor to *Minori* wrote, the poor air, the indoor environment, the long work day, and the clatter of the machines could not compare with "farming under the endless blue sky, in clean air, doing the work as you want to do it."

It was difficult to determine what portion of the women's income went toward household expenditures. For one thing, farm women, especially farm women of Haruko's generation, who were unaccustomed to having large sums of money at their disposal, tended not to keep a budget or records of their daily household expenses. As more and more farmers took wage-paying jobs, however, some kind of record keeping was becoming necessary. Since the practice in the countryside, following urban customs, was for men to turn over all of their money to their wives to manage, the Women's Guild of the Cooperative had recently begun to distribute record ledgers to teach farm women how to maintain household budgets separate from the family's farm records. At a meeting of the Uwa branch of the Women's Guild, a guild leader lectured on the virtues of frugality and disciplined spending. "If you follow a budget," she said, "you will not buy merely what your neighbor buys. Also, if you don't go shopping every day, but only every three or five days, you won't buy so much." Similarly, during the cooking class sponsored by the guild, the instructor slipped in words of advice on budgeting. Women were told first to estimate their income for the coming year and then to apportion their spending as follows: thirty percent for farm equipment, fertilizer, and other farming needs; fifty percent for food, clothing, electricity, telephone, and other household expenses; ten percent for taxes; and the remaining ten percent for savings. If the women followed this advice, said the teacher, they would not overspend. "Budget yourselves," she urged. "Write it down." Haruko asked the instructor to repeat the numbers and hastily scribbled them down, but then forgot what each referred to. "I'm no good at budgeting," she muttered.

The Utsunomiyas were an exception in the sense that Shō-ichi handled money matters: when the family needed money, Shō-ichi withdrew cash from his savings account at the Agricultural Cooperative. He kept most of the vital figures in his head. Writing on the back of a napkin, he estimated that the family's annual income was a little over $10,000—about the average for farmers in Japan. The income from rice was $4,500 and the income from the pig business, in a good year, was $5,600. Government statistics for 1971 showed that, like Shō-ichi, other farmers in the prefecture typically derived sixty to eighty percent of their incomes from nonfarm sources or supplementary farm occupations, such as animal husbandry.*

Shō-ichi's estimate did not include Haruko's earnings, which varied from year to year with the availability of part-time and seasonal work. I calculated that in a good year Haruko might earn as much as $700 or $800, which was in keeping with the average earnings of other farm women. A government survey conducted in 1973 showed that forty percent of all farm women took on outside work, and they earned between $330 and $660 annually.† My own survey in Higashi-uwa county, distributed in the spring of 1975, set the average at about $700, and the head of the local Agricultural Cooperative estimated it to be close to $800.

Why were farm women taking outside jobs? Or, to put it another way, how were their additional earnings used? In the 1973 government survey, sixty percent of the farm women who reported taking on outside work said that they did so in order to pay for the "basic necessities" of life. In my survey of women in the country, fifty percent said they spent most of their earnings on such essentials as food, and another twenty percent said they spent them on clothing for family members and on their children's education. Haruko believed that Bessho women worked not so much to eat as to make extra cash: "Even the wife of the head of Uwa township works."

When I asked Haruko how she spent her own earnings, however, and whether it was really necessary for her to work, I received conflicting responses. "If I had my choice," Haruko said, "I would rather

---

*I am grateful to Ms. Miho Nagata of the Uwa branch of the Farmers Extension Bureau (Nōkyō Kairyō Fukyūshō) for providing this figure.

†Fujin ni kansuru shomondai chōsa kaigi (Conference for investigating various problems concerning women), ed., *Gendai Nihon josei no ishiki to kōdō* (Contemporary Japanese women's attitudes and behavior) (Okurashō [Ministry of Finance]: Tokyo, 1974), p. 267.

spend every day knitting sweaters for the children and straightening up the house." Yet although Shō-ichi said she did not have to take part-time jobs, she would not stay at home. She admitted that she liked having the extra spending money, even if earning it meant exhausting herself and, as she once remarked, not being able to complain, because Shō-ichi had not asked her to do it. It is also true that she worried about having to draw on their savings to pay for the machinery. On several occasions, she even implied that her wage-paying jobs were necessary to cover the cost of the new farm equipment, and Obāsan, sharing this view, commented privately about how sad it was that Haruko had to work.

When I pressed the matter further, I hit a sensitive nerve. Shō-ichi claimed that even without Haruko's earnings their income could cover the monthly payments of about eighty dollars for the machines. "Haruko is a worrier," he said. Haruko retorted that I could not be expected to understand the problem, and Shō-ichi countered, "There is no problem!" Later, however, he modified his position, saying that unless the price of rice increased, women's work would still be necessary to supplement farm income.

It is likely that Haruko worked for a variety of reasons. Her earnings, like those of other farm women, helped the family keep pace with inflation, contributed to mechanization efforts, and also satisfied new consumer desires. It was difficult for anyone to determine in exactly which of these areas expenditure was or was not "necessary." Shō-ichi and Haruko incurred many expenses that reflected the steady erosion of the Japanese farmer's traditional sense of self-sufficiency. Fertilizers, chemical sprays, and electricity and the telephone had become virtual necessities. Gasoline and animal feed, both imported, were among the family's greatest expenses, and these costs were tied to fluctuations in world politics and international trade, so that from one year to the next their incomes rose and fell with little predictability. Shō-ichi had a bad year in 1974, when the American corn crop was damaged and the Middle East oil embargo was imposed. The family's expenses thus varied from year to year, making outside sources of cash imperative.

In addition, the desire for ready-made western-style clothing and for packaged food also drove the Utsunomiyas and other farm families in the area to supplement their farm incomes, making them dependent on the wider economy. Farm women everywhere in Japan, exposed to urban goods and life-styles on television screens, expected more out of their life than their parents' generation did. Haruko was no exception, and her greatest pleasure was shopping for western-style clothing. Yōko wanted the fashionable blue jeans, whose popularity was sweeping the countryside and created jobs for women in blue-jeans factories. Hisashi asked for a record player. Both children preferred packaged white bread to boiled rice for breakfast, and they toasted the bread in a new red electric toaster. The children also expected to go beyond the free junior high school level of education to the high school level, for which tuition fees were charged. Haruko's wages, in other words, went toward attaining a middle-class life-style for her farm family.

Even Obāsan entered the paid labor market, working for a pittance in order to accumulate ready cash of her own. The piecework she did at home for a local factory paid her only one dollar a day for seven or eight hours of knitting pocketbooks. Still, the money enabled her to give cash as birthday gifts to her grandchildren.

In their search for wage-paying jobs, residents of Bessho commuted to Unomachi, if they were lucky enough to find employment there, or they traveled by train to Uwajima, Yawatahama, or even Matsuyama. Almost every woman in Bessho, except those above the age of sixty and mothers of pre-school children, held some kind of part-time job. As a result of this daily exodus, Bessho by day was a ghost town, a bedroom community whose population of children, men, and women emptied into Unomachi early in the morning and headed for schools, jobs, or the railroad station, leaving behind only children under six years of age tended by their grandparents or even great-grandparents, and dogs, caged or tied up outside.

Unlike younger farm women in their late twenties and early thirties, Haruko did not view her income as a passport to independence. It is true she squirreled away her earnings, saving some for old age, spending the rest as she pleased. But for younger women still living in the shadow of their mothers-in-law, possession of one's own money implied something more. One of Haruko's neighbors, who worked part time as a store clerk and lived with her husband's parents, described how she had deliberately lied to her mother-in-law about the sum she had spent on groceries for the household. She told the older woman she had spent less than she actually had, because she did not want to be fully reimbursed from her mother-in-law's purse. That extra amount represented her small measure of economic independence. Other women hearing the story laughed in agreement.

Haruko viewed her position in the family as depending more on her labor than on her wage earnings. Indeed, work itself, rather than her separate though modest pin money, was Haruko's way of ensuring that her voice would be heard. "Do you want to know why I have a say in this family?" she asked one day, angrily interrupting a conversation I was having with one of her friends about the position of Japanese women. "I'll tell you why. Because I work harder than anybody else. It's for that reason that we've been able to increase our landholdings. You saw how my husband was dressed today to attend Yōko's graduation: in a white shirt, a silk tie, and a brown suit. That's the way it's always been. I've done all the work."

Any discussion of Haruko's household work provoked a similar emotional response. Although she felt angry about the way she had been worked in her husband's household, her belief that her status depended on her labor value made her reluctant to allow her mother-in-law to undertake too many household tasks; she seemed to fear that if she were no longer indispensable, her worth might be diminished. Was it perhaps this fear that also made her less than enthusiastic about her husband's mechanization project, even though it promised to free her from some of the most tiring aspects of rice farming? Haruko needed to be needed.

Haruko's anxiety about further investment in machinery, and her resistance to it, also reflected the more general confusion felt in the farming community over the future role of farm women. Would machinery eliminate altogether the need for female labor in the fields or would it simply tie women to other crops, while removing their husbands from the farm? Over one-third of farm women already farmed on their own. Again, would farm households become dependent on the wage labor of women as well as men, and would enough non-agricultural jobs be available?

In the face of these uncertainties, numerous suggestions from various sources floated around the countryside. A speaker addressing the Agricultural Cooperative in Uwa advised women to make more of their own food, as they did in the self-sufficient economy of the past, but then to sell it. And Shō-ichi, who thought it might be profitable for women to stick with farming, suggested that after the harvest they plant rice paddies with cash crops such as tobacco and wheat.

What such proposals had in common was the idea of added reliance on women's work of one sort or another; for during the transitional period at least—while the machines were still new and their efficacy uncertain—women were actually being called upon to perform more functions, rather than fewer. It is not surprising that the almost universal complaint of farm women was lack of sufficient time for rest, for domestic work, and for child care. Moreover, mechanization did not necessarily promise the economic security that would ease the demands on women in the near future. "We have put in machines to do our work," wrote one contributor to *Minori*, "and now we must work to pay for the machines. No sooner do we repay our loans than we have to buy machines. We want binders and automobiles. Our ideals are high, our income is low."

It was understandable that most farm wives envied the comparative leisure enjoyed by their middle-class counterparts in the towns, in their more secure roles as the wives of white-collar salaried men. Even Haruko, though she was perhaps too restless and ambitious to enjoy being anything but busy, nevertheless aspired to the kind of life-style such women represented. Many of her friends were affluent town women whose sole responsibility was homemaking, and perhaps she hoped that by her labor, in farming and in part-time work, she too might one day become, literally, just a housewife.

Haruko's town friends, cheerful and girlish, with graceful, refined manners, seemed to belong to a social class that set them apart from Haruko, who was accustomed to strenuous manual labor and blunt, direct communication. Their fashionable dress (skirts with dainty blouses and cardigan sweaters), their curler-set hairstyles, and their hobbies (raising parakeets and growing prize-winning chrysanthemums) gave evidence of their leisure and affluence. Their lives were so comfortable, in fact, that at least one of the women, in her late thirties, had begun jogging to keep her weight down. All of them wore face cream and powder and had beautiful teeth. (They all used dental floss, whereas Haruko was often too tired at night to give her teeth even a perfunctory brushing.) Because they had no need to take jobs, they had withdrawn into their homes, where they concentrated on being attentive mothers and attractive wives.

One day, one of Haruko's town friends bicycled out to the farm, her skirt gently billowing in the breeze, to get cabbage for her son's pet rabbits. Haruko, dressed in her ankle-high boots, baggy pantaloons, and apron, looked more than ever like a gnome, standing next to her elegant friend and loading the homegrown cabbage heads onto the back of the bicycle. The two women, who lived less than one mile apart, were a study in contrasts, and watching them, it was easier to understand why most farm women, inspired by the middle-class feminine ideal of the housewife, wished they were the wives of salaried men and wanted their own daughters to marry one.

7
Conflict

"LOSING YOUR TEMPER is childish," Haruko said, while discussing an annoying incident that had occurred. "Losing your temper gives your opponent the advantage," Shō-ichi added. "Some men deliberately try to reach your weak points, to make you get angry in order to defeat you in this way. So, I have learned not to get angry, just to laugh."

Displays of hostility and overt conflict are considered unsavory and trivial in village Japan. Marital spats in particular are private concerns in Bessho, where neighbors, pretending not to hear, deliberately stay away from arguing couples. Making outsiders privy to a family altercation would be unthinkable in Japan.

This does not mean that conflict is nonexistent; foreign observers have often marveled at the peacefulness of Japanese communities, but they have wrongly equated the appearance of harmony with the actual existence of it. Conflict within the household does, in fact, exist, but it is carefully disguised, moderated, and expressed in subtle ways. The women especially are apt to suppress angry feelings, but they do not forget them.

I had lived with the Utsunomiya family for several months before I learned how to recognize conflict among family members. My education began one evening after dinner, when Haruko came to my room to apologize for the unpleasantness between herself and her mother-in-law at dinnertime. I was startled by her words, for I had not noticed anything wrong. "What was it about?" I asked.

"A lot of grumbling," Haruko said.

"About what?"

"The rice."

"Didn't she like the taste?"

"It would be better for you not to know," Haruko answered, enigmatically, and left before I could question her further.

I thought about the atmosphere at the dinner table that night, trying to recall what had been said; few words had actually been spoken. Maybe that was the sign I had missed: Haruko and her mother-in-law were not talking to each other. But they rarely did. I remembered what the wife of a local politician had told me about how a woman shows care for other persons by maintaining an easy flow of conversation with them. "It's not gentle or warm enough to say to your mother-in-law, 'Eat some of this.' You should say instead, 'Try this. Wouldn't you like some more?'" I also remembered the sign in front of the Unomachi Town Hall: "A good family has parents and children talking together."

But after twenty years of living and working together, what was there to say? The Japanese do not believe in making dinner conversation: they tend to eat fast and prefer to finish the meal as quickly as possible. Haruko was too busy and tired to ask solicitous questions, and Obāsan did not seem to like idle chatter. Nevertheless, once I had focused on the matter, the silence between Haruko and Obāsan soon became as loud and oppressive to my ears as angry shouting; in particular, Haruko's unwillingness to say a kind word to Obāsan was more effective than any cruel remark she might have made.

Haruko used silence as a weapon. By speaking as little as possible to her mother-in-law, she cut her out of the family fold. The two children, like other teenagers I met in the countryside, were sullen and uncommunicative, absorbed in their homework and television quiz shows. Shō-ichi was frequently away from home, and when he returned, he did not feel obligated to humor his mother or his wife. While Obāsan spoke to him of small daily events, he continued reading the newspaper. Perhaps because she sensed the unimportance of her conversation and the lack of interest on the part of others, her sentences frequently ended in giggles. Even Obāsan's coughing fits at the dinner table, brought on by her failing health, went unremarked.

Only Haruko, in her woman's role as the center of family life, the arbiter and harmonizer of family tensions, was in a position to respond effectively to her mother-in-law's needs, but this she steadfastly refused to do. When Obāsan was out of the house, Haruko would joke, sometimes unfairly, about her mother-in-law's lack of "sense." "She doesn't think the way I do. She's so slow. And she doesn't understand your sense of humor. She can't pick up your nuance. You have to be more straightforward and simple with her. Did you notice she's still being formal with you? 'Would you like some soy sauce?' 'Sorry to take my bath ahead of you.'" Haruko gave a mock shudder as she imitated Obāsan's way of talking to me.

A steady, low-keyed struggle between Haruko and her mother-in-law had been going on for years. Much to Shō-ichi's dismay, most of their discontent with each other was poured into his ears. He said he tried to stay neutral; Haruko said he sided with his mother. The conflicts had largely to do with daily household matters, such as deciding whether to send rice cakes to Shō-ichi's brothers by mail or have them hand-delivered. Haruko resented any interference in the way she ran the home, but Obāsan evidently could not resist. It was her home to which Haruko had come, as a stranger; and Obāsan, as an active farm worker and co-resident, still felt she had certain prerogatives, especially where her own children were concerned. "If her husband were still living," Shō-ichi sighed, "she could complain to him."

The subject of Obāsan was so irritating to Haruko, she was unable to discuss it without getting upset. One outlet for her pent-up feelings was her flower-arrangement class, a group of five or six women, mostly in their forties, who used the class as a forum for their grievances. What they most frequently complained of was parental interference: "I want to try some recipe or I think I'll make some pickles, but before I can do it, my mother-in-law has already done the job."

These women claimed they no longer held back their anger; they had discovered that if they gave vent to feelings of annoyance, the tensions in the air were cleared and they could talk with their mothers-in-law as if nothing had happened. "Being able to get feelings into the open means you are close to a person," said one woman. "You are no longer strangers. You are close enough to be able to argue and after you argue, you feel closer still."

Of course they had not behaved so freely when they were first married. As young brides, when they had not yet established their positions in the households of their husbands' parents, they had felt more constraints on the expression of anger and they had relieved their feelings by talking to friends or sisters. Some had tried to cheer themselves by going shopping, and others had slipped off to a place where nobody could see them, like the toilet, and cried. Some of the hamlet women spoke of aching in their shoulders and chest caused by emotional distress. All agreed that the ability to argue with one's family, and to be open and not stand on ceremony, was a sign of closeness: you don't argue with outsiders any more than you impose on them. When your husband calls, "Hey, bring me some tea," he is conveying this sense of a close relationship.

The younger wives, according to Haruko, asserted themselves from the very beginning of their marriage: "They say to their husband's mother, 'You do it one way, I do it another. I'll do it the way I want.'" Haruko herself, after almost twenty years of marriage, had not reached even this stage of accommodation with her mother-in-law. The mere mention of Obāsan drove her into a rage. Sneering and snorting, she would imitate Obāsan's oppressive manner and excessive politeness.

"I can't stand my mother-in-law," Haruko blurted out one night, when the rest of the family was already asleep. "I hate the way she's always creeping around the house, creep creep. She's so mousy. You never know what she's really thinking; she holds back her true feelings, so you can't tell if she's harboring ill will against you and, if she is, why."

"But Obāsan has praised you to me," I replied. It seemed to me that Obāsan genuinely appreciated her daughter-in-law's contribution to the family and also understood her high-strung personality.

Haruko tensed and insisted that Obāsan's words of praise were a sham. She began talking faster and faster, while stuffing food in her mouth, leaning over the *kotatsu* and sucking the juice from tangerines, then tossing the skins on the floor. She downed a glass of wine and followed that with a shot of whiskey, swallowed in one gulp. As she normally did not drink whiskey, I became alarmed and tried to change the subject.

It was almost one o'clock in the morning, well beyond Haruko's usual hour for retiring. Groggy from lack of sleep, she rambled on, repeating herself. Finally, in the middle of a sentence, she fell over on the floor, murmured "I must go to bed," and stumbled into her bedroom.

Although I felt sorry for Obāsan, I also sympathized with Haruko's desire to be independent, and I had to admit that, like Haruko, I found her presence oppressive. It took many weeks before I felt that Obāsan had truly accepted me into the family. Although she never said much to me—that was the problem—somehow her behavior led me to believe she disapproved of my being there or perhaps disapproved of my idle existence. From her point of view, all I did was sit around reading, writing, and worst of all, talking. Did she realize that talking—asking questions, acquiring information—was my work? Probably not. Besides, in all truth, I felt self-conscious about my scholar's life-style, and more than a little guilty about studying while the other adults in the family did manual labor.

Obāsan's attitude toward me changed at New Year's time when Haruko, who usually discouraged all my efforts to help her, was so busy she accepted my offer to pitch in with the annual household cleaning. I was given a smocklike apron to don and, wrapping my hair in a kerchief, as I had seen other women do, together with Yōko I began to scrub the tile in the bathroom, dust the frames around the *shoji*, and mop the stone kitchen floor. Shō-ichi was exhilarated to see me in my woman's work outfit and Obāsan was first surprised, then impressed with my performance. Perhaps I was imagining it, but from that time on, Obāsan treated me with a new respect: I had won my stripes by doing traditional women's work.

After that time Obāsan began praising me in front of guests, saying that I was good at remembering what people told me. She also spoke approvingly of how the family had begun communicating more with each other since I had come: I had initiated conversation and the children were joining in. She was glad about this. One day she suggested that I study in Yōko's room, because it was warmer.

Obāsan nevertheless felt free to express disapproval, however mild, of my behavior: she told me one night, for example, to go to bed as soon as possible, because the light was bothering her daughter-in-law, who was trying to sleep. (As soon as Obāsan left, Haruko came out of her bedroom, laughed, and sat down with me to watch television.) When Obāsan told me it was just as well I was leaving in May, because during the summer the family would be pressed for time, I realized how blunt she could be. She abhorred waste and criticized me for my habit of leaving food unfinished. Looking with disgust at the half cup of cold instant coffee I had left on the table, she remarked that "even Mr. Shoya," a wealthy *sake*-brewer and the former landlord of almost all the farmers in the six hamlets that ringed the rice plain, "never wastes a grain of rice."

If Obāsan felt free to correct my behavior, she also became more willing to ask me, discreetly, about the comings and goings of other members in our household, and particularly of Haruko. Because part of my research consisted of observing Haruko at her daily tasks, or at least knowing what her plans were for the day, I had inadvertently become the family's central intelligence officer. It frequently came as a surprise to discover that Obāsan, who lived across the road and took all her meals with us, was not informed of the ups and downs and occasional dramas that punctuated the daily routine in our household. "Has my daughter-in-law gone to town?" she would say, slipping silently into the kitchen while I sat alone, eating breakfast.

I usually answered with all the details I could muster, like a scout faithfully relaying the latest reconnaissance reports: "Yes, she went to buy kimono material. She left only a few minutes ago. She said she would walk to town. I think she wants to make a summer kimono for Yōko. Your son is feeding the pigs."

"Oh," is all Obāsan would ever say.

I do not know whether Haruko deliberately neglected to inform her mother-in-law of family events, or even whether she was conscious of doing so, but the effect of her negligence was unmistakable:

uninformed, Obāsan was less than a full member of the family. Information, however trivial, was power for these two women, each attempting to exercise her authority over the other in domestic affairs. By keeping Obāsan uninformed, Haruko was in a sense preventing her from participating in family life and in particular from interfering in Haruko's daily decisions, from telling her what she could and could not do.

That Obāsan, for her part, felt that her role as mother-in-law carried with it certain rights of interference and supervision was suggested by a conversation she had one day with Haruko's brother. Haruko had failed to tell Obāsan of her father's serious operation. She disliked her father and had not gone to visit him in Uwajima when he first entered the hospital there. When Haruko's brother stopped by the house, Obāsan, apologizing profusely, explained she had not known his father was so ill. "Please don't think I told Haruko she couldn't go to the hospital," she said. Haruko's brother, embarrassed, protested that such a thought had never entered his head, but Obāsan repeated over and over that if Haruko had not gone to the hospital, it was not because she had prevented her from going. Obāsan's apology reflected a complete misreading of the relationship she had with her daughter-in-law.

Although it was clear that Obāsan would like to have been called upon to supervise, she nevertheless understood well enough that her own view of her role in the family was shared by neither Haruko nor Shō-ichi. Such advice and criticism as she had to offer concerning family matters, she confided to me, a stranger.

One cold winter day, Hisashi agreed to accompany his father on the overnight watch at the mountain pig pens. No one had thought to inform Obāsan. They left by car at nine o'clock, traveling icy roads in the midst of snow flurries. Two hours later they still had not reached the mountain camp and Haruko grew alarmed. Finally, Shō-ichi telephoned to report that the car engine had stalled, and they had had to borrow boots for Hisashi and walk three miles in the snow to the camp. Vastly relieved, Haruko nevertheless worried out loud about Hisashi who, not quite recovered from a cold, had left without hat, gloves, or muffler.

The next morning, Obāsan, still unaware of her grandson's absence, summoned him for a telephone call. Informed by me of his whereabouts and of the previous night's adventure, she said, "My daughter-in-law told me nothing." Seeing Hisashi's gloves and hat lying on the table, she realised that he had forgotten to take them and muttered, "My, how terrible!" and then, "His mother wasn't careful enough. She was careless." Before I could answer, she added, "If I were to say something, I'd be criticized."

On another occasion Obāsan confided to me her concern about several young men in Bessho who she thought were being disloyal to Shō-ichi. Although he had helped them get to the United States to study farming and guided the agrarian reforms, which would benefit everybody in the area, they had joined the Liberal-Democratic party and campaigned for that party's gubernatorial candidate, in opposition to the Socialist party candidate Shō-ichi supported. One reason for their disloyalty, she suggested, was that the Liberal-Democratic party offered them money to take a study trip to the Philippines. "They forgot their *on*" (their sense of obligation), she said. "I hate that sort of person. My son never talks about it. But I know." Then she added, "I'm not listened to because I am old." Just at that point, we heard Shō-ichi's car pull up to the house. "Don't say anything more," Obāsan whispered. "He's back."

Toward the end of my stay, Obāsan began confiding in me even more openly. "My daughter-in-law's insistence on doing all the work by herself is a bad trait," she said once, sadly. "It makes me feel bad." She had come through the kitchen holding a laundry basket containing her clothes and stood in front of me still holding the basket as she talked.

"If I say, 'Let me do that for you' or 'Shall I take care of that?' Haruko snaps 'It's already done.'" Obāsan imitated Haruko's abrupt way of replying. "I'd be glad if she'd let me help her. It would please me. And then if she would say a kind word of thanks—that would also please me."

Haruko, meanwhile, seemed determined to do as much housework as possible by herself, without her mother-in-law's help. This was not to spare Obāsan so much as to keep her out of the way. Although Obāsan was responsible for washing the dinner dishes, Haruko usually tried to do this task, too, even after a day spent farming. Now and then Obāsan was called upon to stay with the children, and she was always on hand to fix dinner when Haruko could not return home on time. On these rare occasions Obāsan prepared only very simple meals of raw fish and rice. The reason Haruko gave for not having her mother-in-law cook dinner more often was her lack of familiarity with the western recipes preferred by the children, such as spaghetti or fried chicken.

One of the only other tasks regularly assigned to Obāsan was preparing the pigs' gruel by boiling leftover table scraps, potatoes, packaged seeds, and water in an enormous iron cauldron in the shed behind the house. When both Shō-ichi and Haruko were detained, Obāsan also fed the pigs. She did all her tasks, however minor (weeding the goldfish pond, washing carrots at the outdoor faucet, and the like), with willingness, pleased to be needed. Yet Haruko, perhaps still trying to prove her worth in her husband's home by dint of her own hard labor, resisted delegating work to her mother-in-law. She never forgot how, when she was bedridden with asthma over ten years before, her mother-in-law, though sympathetic, had complained about having to hire help during the harvest season. Hard word was Haruko's trademark, her way of justifying her membership in her husband's family, and because everyone else relied on her, Haruko's work was a source of power. The price she paid, however, was a frenzied daily pace.

Obāsan seemed to sense the reason behind Haruko's exertions. One night, after Haruko and Shō-ichi had rushed to the hospital to see Haruko's father, who had taken a turn for the worse, Obāsan said that Haruko should have gone earlier, as soon as her father entered the hospital. I defended Haruko by saying her head was still hurting from the accident she had while working on the construction team.

Surprised, Obāsan said she thought Haruko had already fully recovered from the accident. "Yesterday she went out all alone to pick *warabi* [edible bracken]. I could have helped her. She went there instead of going to the hospital. I didn't know she wanted *warabi*. Sometimes I feel I'm doing unnecessary work." Seeing Obāsan on her hands and knees a few days later weeding the path in front of the house, I asked her why she bothered to weed an area in which nothing was planted. "It's dirty," was all she replied. Perhaps this is what she meant by "unnecessary work."

Whereas Haruko detested her mother-in-law's lack of candor and her formality, Haruko's own daughter, Yōko, was bothered by Haruko's overly energetic mothering and her bossiness and indiscretion. A case in point was the way she treated a young college student home on vacation, who had stopped by to visit and to practice speaking English with me. Haruko suggested that we sit in the living room so we could be alone. She then urged Yōko to join us and take advantage of the opportunity to practice her own English. Just as the three of us had settled down, Haruko brought out coffee and plopped down at the table with us to look through recent family photographs. Every few minutes she interrupted the young man in Japanese, saying to him, urgently, "Drink your coffee before it gets cold." Or, "Don't you want some sugar?"

Suddenly, she put down the pictures and made a telephone call, chatting in a loud voice while I tried to get our guest to understand what I had just said. At last, hanging up the receiver, Haruko took the pencil we were using to write out English words and began marking down the pictures she wanted to have duplicated. At this point, Yōko could no longer contain her irritation. "Mother, how annoying. Don't bother us. Leave us alone!"

But Haruko could not understand what she had done wrong. A few minutes later, having dragged her daughter into our conversation, she nagged her to take a bath. Yōko, infuriated by her mother's unrelenting interference, punched her on the arm.

Oblivious of her daughter's exasperation and the reasons for it, Haruko now began nagging her to study. Our guest slipped away, and shortly afterward Shō-ichi returned home, whereupon Haruko began complaining that Yōko had not done her homework. Responding to the injustice of her mother's complaint, Yōko, who clearly felt no constraints on expressing her feelings, countered by giving an accurate and even amusing blow-by-blow imitation of how Haruko had badgered the guest as he tried to concentrate on our English conversation. Shō-ichi, accustomed to tension between the female generations in the family, smiled and remained silent, and the atmosphere quickly eased as we all turned to looking at the pictures on the table and joking.

But Yōko's clash with her mother had apparently taken its toll on her. A few minutes later, emerging from the bath, she fainted. She had suffered three or four fainting spells like this in less than a year, and although the exact cause had not been diagnosed, a doctor who was a longtime friend of the family suggested when Shō-ichi phoned him that night that they could be caused by "nerves," or possibly eyestrain. Ignoring the possible psychological cause, Haruko took Yōko to an eye doctor the following day, but the examination showed that her vision was perfectly normal, and the incident was soon forgotten.

Some family arguments were about me. From the beginning of my stay in their household, Haruko and Shō-ichi clashed over how best to serve my interests. Occasionally, Obāsan jumped into the fray to protect me from being exploited, as she saw it, by the demands of others. She chided Haruko for pushing me into a speaking engagement at the junior high school when I had a cold. But when Haruko sanctioned the idea of my taking photographs at a funeral, she was scandalized. Haruko, in a slow, patronizing voice, told her mother-in-law that photographing the funeral would be "helpful" to my work. Obāsan smiled gently, swallowing her objections.

Mother-in-law and daughter-in-law did agree on at least one issue. Both were opposed to any further political involvement on Shō-ichi's part. When the Socialist party approached Shō-ichi about running for office in the upcoming gubernatorial elections, Haruko was unyielding in her opposition, and she and Shō-ichi frequently argued over what his decision should be. Haruko still recalled with some bitterness how for much of their married life, while Shō-ichi served on the town assembly, attending meetings during the day and often away from home, she had handled childrearing and farming almost entirely alone. "She worked her fingers to the bone," Obāsan said, taking her daughter-in-law's side.

Now in the last days of December, Shō-ichi was once again considering political office, though this time his party had no chance of success: it simply wanted to have a candidate in the race. Shō-ichi's candidacy thus represented a complete sacrifice of time, money, and energy. "I was raised to sacrifice for the emperor," he explained, "and now I am working for society."

Haruko remained adamantly opposed. Her concerns were day-to-day practical matters directly related to her family, and her down-to-earth, commonsensical approach to life was just the opposite of her husband's romantic idealism. "My husband is passionate and emotional. He can cry over a television movie. I'm coldhearted."

Yet, if she opposed her husband's wishes, it was not because she failed to sympathize with his dilemma; it was simply that she refused to allow him to place the needs of party or society ahead of his family's needs. She was committed to promoting the family's interests, and was accordingly prepared to work slavishly for a better life for all of them; but she was unwilling to sacrifice for a larger, more elusive good.

For two weeks they argued doggedly whether Shō-ichi should enter the election. One day, finding him asleep at home in the middle of the day, Haruko whispered, "He's trying to think things out." When a group of supporters came to the house later in the week to urge him to run and to persuade Haruko to agree, she sneaked out the side door, mounted her motor scooter, and, without telling anybody where she was going, sought refuge for the evening in the nearby home of her sister. Obāsan sided with Haruko and finally, a few days afterward, Shō-ichi gave in.

"My political career is finished," he told Haruko morosely. "To refuse even to try is to be totally defeated. I feel as though I have died."

Haruko replied, softly, "I'm sorry I bent your will."

"I didn't give in because of you," her husband answered. "I was worried about what would happen to the pig business."

Haruko was nonetheless elated and relieved.

8
Home and School

YŌKO AND HISASHI were studious children, and Haruko pushed them in their studies, hoping they would qualify for college. Only about one-third of Uwa's high school graduates enter college, and those who do tend to take agriculture, nursing, or teaching degrees. Shō-ichi had always hoped his son would follow in his footsteps—in fact, the characters he chose to write Hisashi's name mean "long-continued"—but Haruko expected both children to leave farming in favor of salaried jobs. She also wanted to be independent of them in her old age. "It's been a Japanese custom to have your children live with you in your old age to take care of you," she said, "but I don't want this. My husband is different. He would like to live close to his son, he says, so he can drink *sake* with him and advise him. But I would like to live with my husband alone and enjoy our hobbies. I want to have our own income and property. For this, we have to start saving money."

It was perhaps Haruko's quest for independence for herself and her children, combined with her busy work routine, that explained the children's lack of social manners and the communication gap between them and their elders. They ignored guests, took no initiative in family matters, and failed to respond to parental requests. Candy wrappers were dropped on the floor and presents flung carelessly on top of the television, in flagrant violation of the strict norms of Japanese behavior and etiquette.

"Parents lack confidence," explained a friend of Haruko's, a vice-president of the Uwa Parent-Teacher Association. "Also, parents want to recognize their children's freedom." Shō-ichi added that parents had lost confidence in themselves on account of reforms in the schools' ethics courses since the American Occupation, which had replaced the traditional values of filial piety and obedience with democratic teachings that seemed to give official sanction to assertiveness. Shō-ichi's concern about the effects of the current value system was shared by others in the community. As one woman in her sixties remarked, "Young people are getting selfish. They misunderstand the word *democracy* and think it means freedom and selfishness."

Although in Haruko's eyes Shō-ichi was a strict disciplinarian because he refused to buy the children all the things they wanted, he never followed up his requests with firm action when the children disobeyed him. While we were having dinner one night with a friend of mine visiting from Tokyo, Yōko sat in the same room, calling her friends on the phone and talking in a loud voice. Twice Shō-ichi told her to get off the phone and finally he complained to Haruko, who repeated his request, but to no avail. On another occasion, when Hisashi left the dinner table in the middle of the meal, Shō-ichi called him back with a loving smile on his face, but Hisashi ignored him, went to his room, and started practicing his guitar.

The exemplar of traditional manners in the family was the children's grandmother, who had not been influenced by the democratic values that swept over Haruko and Shō-ichi's generation immediately after the war. Yet her no-nonsense, puritanical and self-disciplined approach to life had only a limited effect on her grandchildren, who saw their own mother disregard her words and therefore had little motivation to behave differently. Obāsan rarely spoke. For the most part, she "knew her place," and she hovered on the fringes of family life. When Shō-ichi and Haruko were home, she retired early after dinner to her house across the road, where she had her own black-and-white television set. When the children were left alone, however, she sat with them around the *kotatsu* in the main house and occasionally corrected their manners, usually when they failed to show proper courtesy toward me. "Offer her some of the *yōkan*," she would say, as they monopolized the jellied sweet before them. "Say yes promptly" (if I asked for a small favor). She spoke quietly, and with a refined vocabulary and an air of civility that contrasted sharply with Haruko's blunter speech.

It was the same in other homes in the countryside. The grand-mothers of Japan appear to be the sole guardians of the manners of rural Japanese teenagers in the home. Visiting a farm family in Ake-hama, I observed the seventy-five-year-old grandmother instruct her twenty-year-old granddaughter in basic good manners. The old woman, with only one tooth remaining in her mouth, told her how to reply to my greetings. "Say 'Excuse me.' Thank her for the gifts she sent recently." The girl, shy and embarrassed in my presence, re-mained silent. Later the grandmother told her to offer me some lunch.

"We do not have time for ourselves or to help our children," one farm woman told me. "We do not have much communication with our children, who are completely in the hands of teachers and tele-vision." Her remark was applicable to Haruko and Shō-ichi's chil-dren as well. Before I joined the family, the children did not eat with their parents, but took their meals separately in front of the television. After my arrival, although they began eating with the family, they gulped down their food and left the table ahead of everybody else. Sometimes they had to be wrenched away from the television, and often they fell asleep in front of it, under the blanket that covered the *kotatsu*.

The children's behavior on certain occasions seemed to be dictated less by rudeness than by a desire to block adult efforts to flatter them or otherwise make them the center of attention. When Shō-ichi be-gan praising Yōko's academic record, she called him "bothersome," meaning she did not want the flattery, and when Shō-ichi asked his son to play his guitar, Hisashi replied curtly, "I don't want to." Nei-ther child wanted to be placed in the limelight.

Hisashi, aged twelve, was withdrawn and babyish, and because his parents still considered him a child, they expected nothing of him in the way of household chores. He left his underwear on the floor of the dressing room instead of in the laundry basket, and he regularly knocked down the towel rack and left the damp towels lying in a heap. Hisashi was tall for his age and very thin. He wore dungarees and a blue Eisenhower-style jacket with United States Army insignia on the sleeve. Only once or twice in six months did friends come to the house; for the most part he occupied himself by playing endless rounds of ping-pong alone, strumming his guitar, and watching television cartoons with fairy-tale or science-fiction themes. Though he was in his last term of primary school, he was clearly still a child.

Yōko, who was a little over three years older, seemed more adult. At five feet, two inches, she was taller than the other women in her family and almost as tall as her father. She was also heavier than average, with a broad bone structure and dark complexion that greatly distressed her. "I am very, very, very fat," she wrote, in English, to her Philippine pen pal. In her New Year's cards to girlfriends, she drew a rabbit (the Oriental zodiac sign for 1975) and had the rabbit say, "I wish I were white and thinner." Yōko's solid physical presence, together with her husky laugh—a loud ha-ha rather than a feminine giggle—and her talent for identifying Japanese athletes on the television screen gave her a certain air of tomboyishness. Yōko enjoyed singing and was learning to play the drums and flute at school. She also showed a talent for drawing cartoonlike sketches, mainly of girls in western-style clothing, who had a Caucasian look about them of the sort cultivated by Japanese movie stars.

Yōko was in her final year of junior high school, and she was ambitious and energetic in her studies. In the evening she was occupied mainly with her homework and with preparing for her entrance examination for senior high school. (Senior high school is not compulsory in Japan, and in addition to passing an entrance examination, students must pay a tuition fee.) Although ninety-five percent of the applicants pass the examinations, they must nevertheless invest many grueling weeks of study in them, and Yōko, armed with a thermos of hot water and a jar of instant coffee, frequently worked late into the night. Eventually, she hoped, she would enter a teachers' college.

Yōko was rarely expected to assist in house or farm chores, though occasionally, when her mother was ailing, she did the laundry in the washing machine, and several times she cooked spaghetti, her special forte. Unlike Haruko, she was not raised to be a farm woman. Ha-

Hisashi in his school uniform.

Yōko on her way to school.

ruko might claim to enjoy farming on her own account, but like other
farm wives she was adamant about not wanting her daughter to farm
and a little wistful about not having herself married an office worker
or some other salaried man. Once, when Shō-ichi was away, Yōko was
asked to run water in the pig troughs. It was evident that she did not
take easily to such tasks, for one of the pigs frightened her when it
tried to climb out of its enclosure, and she returned to the house without shutting off the water. That evening, her grandmother reported
standing ankle-deep in water to feed the pigs. As Yōko wept, Haruko
silently finished preparing dinner, then put on her rubber boots,
picked up a flashlight, and returned with Obāsan to the pigsty to
sweep out the water. There they found a dead pig and dragged it out
of the sty by its feet. None of this work seemed to distress the two
women: Haruko came back to the house, finished her meal, bathed,
washed her hair, and then, with her hair in curlers, telephoned a
friend to chat.

Farm parents say their children are spoiled and self-willed, but a
more accurate description is perhaps isolated or withdrawn. Children have two separate worlds, school and home, with no enduring
bridge between the two in the form of visits from school friends or
evening social events at the school. The sole tenuous links between
school and home are the report card and the PTA.

The report card comes three times a year, and it invites parents'
comments. Yōko's report card was of the standard kind. It listed her
attainments in all nine of her courses: in Japanese, English, society,
home economics, music, mathematics, art, science, and physical education–personal hygiene. Grades were awarded on a ten-point scale,
and overall Yōko scored in the top ten percent in her class. The report
card also recorded Yōko's absences, her general progress, her behavior (which was assessed with an A–B letter grade), and her likes and
dislikes, and it evaluated her basic character traits, under such head-
ings as leadership qualities, self-reliance, cooperativeness, fairness,
public-spiritedness, and originality. In the space reserved for parents'
comments, Shō-ichi had written, "Be as strict as you can. I leave her
in your hands."

The other link between home and school is the PTA, whose name is written in English letters. Haruko said that everybody with school-age children must join. Although most members are mothers, the president, chosen by the other members, is always a man. The executive board consisted of three men and three women, and there were two vice-presidents, one a woman and one a man. Among other things, the PTA supports recreational facilities for the children, and it collects money for the children's school lunches. It also sponsors an Open School Day, on which parents observe classes and talk to teachers about their children's progress. The association has no part in decisions about the curriculum, however; the curriculum is entirely the responsibility of education officials, and textbooks are prescribed by the regional office of the Ministry of Education.

Though the report card and the Open School Day sponsored by the PTA offer parents the opportunity to keep up with their children's progress at school and to voice their opinions, most are content simply to defer to the authority of the teachers. In fact at one Open School Day I attended, the parents seemed almost to be intimidated by their children's teachers, and such questions as they raised had largely to do with their own role as parents rather than with the students' academic life in the schools. In one room, the teacher sat in front of the mothers, who formed a half circle, squirmed, looked embarrassed, and stared into their laps. Unaccustomed to voicing their opinions in public and particularly in front of teachers, the women were further intimidated by my presence. When Shō-ichi explained that I wanted to sit in on the discussion, one woman gasped, covered her mouth with her hand, said *Hazukashii* ("I feel shy"), and playfully slapped her neighbor on the arm. It was several minutes before anybody volunteered to talk. Finally one woman spoke up. Television was a big problem in her home, she confessed. "My children watch television after school and all evening. If I try to say something to them, they answer, 'Be quiet!'" Other mothers murmured their agreement, and the teacher advised fixing a time limit on television watching.

The woman's concern that her children devote sufficient time to their studies was a typical one. The parents' role, as most parents see it, is to supply the nagging to set their children to work at their studies, and to ensure that they are free of distractions and of demands to help with the running of the farm, a luxury they themselves could not afford when they were young. "Times have changed a great deal," Haruko said, recalling how her own father would not allow her to study for examinations during the harvesting and planting seasons and scolded her for studying instead of working in the fields. "Nowadays, children are urged by their parents to study, and as long as they study, the parents are satisfied."

School is in session in Japan 240 days out of the year, and the children attend classes five and one-half days a week. The schools give many children their first dose of the discipline that is lacking in their home lives. In junior high school, for example, children learn to rise when their teacher enters the room and to remain standing until told to sit down. Boys are required to wear crew cuts and uniforms of navy blue trousers and jackets; girls are forbidden to polish their nails or get permanent waves, and they must also wear navy blue uniforms: skirts and middy blouses. Both sexes also confront a number of prohibitions on unsupervised social activities: they may not go without adults to movie theaters, coffee shops, or bowling alleys.

The principal of the Uwa middle school, echoing contemporary values, claimed he was trying to develop a spirit of independence in his students. One example of what he meant was the annual school fair, run entirely by students, who set up booths publicizing their extracurricular clubs and performed at a school assembly. One boy, pounding on a lectern, did a humorous imitation of one of his teachers, to the delight of his laughing schoolmates. Seated on one side of the auditorium, the principal and the teachers looked on impassively.

After meeting several school principals in a round of ritual greetings, I could only wonder whether one of the qualifications for the job was not the ability to look weighty. Crusty, jowly men in their fifties, they were treated like dignitaries and accorded numerous prerogatives, including large offices with at least two leather chairs (white lace doilies on the backs of them), a coffee table, and a young female clerk who was quick to bring tea and cake for guests. The men displayed a somber countenance that suggested they were not the kind of people one would want to cross. Indeed, a female mathematics and science teacher at one school claimed that she and other members of the teachers' union were discriminated against by being denied salary increases, and they had filed a class action suit.

An appearance I made at the junior high school taught me a little about the discipline school administrators expected of their energetic charges, and reminded me about the Japanese attention to rituals of social intercourse. Having been invited to speak to the students, I prepared a variation on what had become my stock speech (originally suggested by Haruko) about my parents' sacrifices for my education. It was a winning sermon.

Arriving at the school, I was immediately ushered into the principal's office. The kerosene stove was lit, the pretty young female clerk brought green tea on a round tray, and the principal made light conversation from across a small table. After a short while, he escorted me to the school gym, where I realized with a start that the entire student population—776 students, all dressed in identical navy blue uniforms, the boys with their hair closely cropped—had been waiting with their teachers for fifteen or twenty minutes while we had been drinking our tea.

As we approached the door, a photographer suddenly appeared and snapped our picture, while the vice-principal stepped up to the microphone and barked a command. The students sat up in their seats. Another command: the students rose in unison. Another command: they bowed.

The principal escorted me across the gym to a table on the other side, left me sitting there by myself, walked back to a table near the door, and sat down next to several of the teachers. The vice-principal then introduced the principal, who walked slowly to the foot of the stairs leading to the stage, bowed to me, walked up to the steps and bowed to the Japanese flag hanging like a backdrop, turned to face the students, who by now were seated again, and, after a significant pause, bowed to them. They instantly returned the bow. A brief introduction and I was on stage.

After my talk, the principal asked me a complicated question concerning my opinion of university students' thought. He was obliquely referring to radical tendencies among young people in their college years. Students in the audience were more interested in my opinion of Japanese television shows, and they also asked whether the scenery in Japan was similar to that in the United States. One student asked me whether I thought students should be given more time between classes to move from one classroom to another—the current controversial issue at the school.

At last I was allowed to return to my table at the far side of the gym. The principal reiterated in two sentences the theme of my speech, seizing on a comment I had made at the end about the need for Japan to find its own way and not imitate the United States. The vice-principal again barked his command, the students stood, and the principal crossed the room, escorting me out to the sound of heavy applause.

Back in his office, the principal ordered more tea and Japanese cakes, in the shape of plums and individually wrapped in real leaves that I almost ate. He also gave me an envelope containing 3,000 yen (about ten dollars)—an unexpected honorarium. With these obligations out of the way, he sat back in his chair and asked me whether I could tell the difference between a Japanese and a Chinese. He could not tell an Englishman and a Frenchman apart, he confided, adding that Japanese had yellow skins, halfway between white and black. "Japanese tend to look down on blacks," he informed me, "but to look up to whites." What was the point he was trying to make, I wondered dully.

Warming to the idea of cultural differences, he was soon discoursing on the subject of cultural change and began to bemoan the loss of traditional Japanese morality. Distinctions between the sexes had disappeared, he asserted. The Japanese had become materialistic. The number of Buddhist altars in people's houses was decreasing, and this meant the tradition of offering thanks was also disappearing.

When the principal finally drove me home in his late-model white Toyota sedan, Obāsan, who was weeding by the side of the road and whose education had stopped after the sixth grade, looked impressed. Yōko, hearing my account of meeting him, said he gave his Buddhist altar speech several times a year.

PART III
Farm Community

9
Fumiko, the Genteel Farm Woman

I FIRST MET HER during the autumn harvest festival in a remote hamlet that we reached after a winding thirty-minute drive from Bessho, passing waterfalls and gushing streams along the way. The hamlet was a picturesque cluster of twenty or thirty black-tile-roof houses nestled in the side of the mountain. It was exquisitely beautiful and so too was the woman, but her refined manners seemed curiously out of place in these rustic surroundings.

She spoke a clear, unaccented Japanese that set her apart from the other farm women in the area, who spoke in the local dialect; and her curly, professionally set hair, her elegant kimono, and her delicate features suggested urban wealth and aristocratic breeding. She handled the awkwardness of my presence with ease and charm: unlike other women in the countryside, who were inclined to laugh nervously, turn away shyly, or stare silently when they first met me, afraid I would not understand them and not knowing what to say to me, she spoke slowly and carefully and even slipped in one or two English words to grease the wheels of conversation and set me at ease.

What was she doing here among the drying rice stacks? In my mental picture of her, she belonged in a villa in Kyoto, and not where I first saw her, behind a low table heaped with platters of food, quietly dishing out raw fish, slices of apple, and soybean pastries for the male guests in her house. Only her hands betrayed her occupation: they were chapped and red, with short, stubby fingers—the hands of a farm woman. And when I looked closer, I noticed that half of the middle finger of her right hand was missing.

The men spoke mainly about business. Our host, urging me to eat, piled my plate with food, and his mother, a heavy-set woman in her late sixties, tried to entertain me by bringing out wedding pictures of her two married sons, then a map of Japan, and finally a flyswatter. I wanted to talk further with the genteel lady, as I had silently dubbed her, but I was distracted by a question one of the other guests asked me, and when I looked around, she and her mother-in-law were gone.

As we were leaving, she reappeared and I blurted out something about wanting to see her again, to talk to her. I feared I had been too aggressive, but two days later she phoned to invite me to her home, and ten days after that, excited by the prospect of photographing the hamlet and learning more about the mysterious lady, I returned for a weekend at her house.

Her name was Fumiko and she was thirty-six years old. She did all the farming alone, except during harvest season, when one or two male workers were hired to help carry the sixty-pound sacks of rice. Her husband, a red-faced, roly-poly man with a raspy voice and a small, pointed beard, was the president of a prosperous construction company inherited from his father, who still legally owned it and paid him a salary. His company had profited from the recent intro- duction of mechanized farming into the region by expanding its dealings to include the sale as well as the operation of heavy equip- ment to build roads and bulldoze fields, and he was occupied seven days a week, managing three separate offices and forty laborers.

From the first day of her married life, Fumiko had lived with her in-laws. The household in those days had consisted of her husband's parents, his two unmarried younger brothers, and his sister. Fumiko's mother-in-law had undergone surgery for a stomach ailment and could no longer work; she stayed in bed all morning. The sister, who remained at home for many years before marrying at the unusually late age of thirty-two, helped care for her mother and also went to sewing classes. Since all the men in the family were engaged full time in the family business, the full burden of farming had fallen on Fumiko, as the eldest son's bride.

Fumiko was expected not only to do all the farm work alone, but also to prepare all the meals, including box lunches, for the six family members and herself. Her days began at four in the morning, when she stoked the fire and drew water from the well, and ended at midnight: she had only four hours of sleep. "I was worked like a slave," she said.

The family's house was over one hundred and fifty years old and essentially had not changed since the time it was built. One exception was the black tile roof, which had replaced the original straw-thatched one. Another was the kitchen, which in Fumiko's early years of married life had been outside the house, but was now connected to it and was equipped with a sink with running water, a small refrigerator, and two gas burners. The original sink—a large stone tub resting on the floor—still remained, as did the old wood-burning stove. Two basin-shaped holes on top of the stove had served as burners for cooking rice in the old days. Now one of the holes was covered with a piece of wood, and over the other one rested a modern rice cooker attached to a gas line. But despite the improvements, the kitchen, facing northeast and resting on a stone floor, remained cold and inconvenient.

When Fumiko entered the household, as a young bride of nineteen, she experienced acute loneliness. Her husband's siblings, while still living at home, formed a "family group" that excluded her, she said. She was a stranger to them. She learned to farm only after her marriage, and having to work alone left her feeling even more isolated than other young farm women, whose in-laws and husband worked with them in the fields. In addition, Fumiko's gentility was in all likelihood viewed with suspicion in a farm household that regarded daughters-in-law, in the traditional way, as additional labor power and servants for the older generation. Finally, Fumiko said, her husband never sided with her if her mother-in-law criticized her. This may have been because he was himself financially dependent on his parents, but also because he was genuinely attached to them, and especially to his mother, whom he closely resembled in looks and personality.

Fumiko had not expected to marry so young, nor had she wanted to marry the man chosen for her. She had hoped to go to college, but shortly after she graduated from high school, her mother was taken ill and the family could no longer support Fumiko's education. Against her wishes, in 1957 her grandfather arranged for her to marry his brother's grandson—her second cousin. "I did not care for him when I first saw his picture, but since they were related to us, we couldn't call it off. At that time I cared for another man. He later graduated from college and became a dentist. But his family was different in status from mine and, besides, I lacked a college education. So I resigned myself to fate. My younger sister had the chance to date the man chosen for her, but I didn't."

Her father had become a farmer only after the war; earlier he had been a police officer, and the family had enjoyed a certain prestige. When Fumiko was three years old, he was assigned to the Japanese colony of Manchuria. A picture taken sometime in the late nineteen-thirties showed him wearing a long sword and sitting astride a handsome white horse. War and defeat forced the family to return to Japan, where the pressure of the times brought severe hardships, and they managed to survive by eating mainly potatoes. Finally, her father bought some land and turned to farming. His inner faith had sustained him through the family's trials, Fumiko explained. "He reads a lot. And his inner life is rich. I too try to be content and to cultivate my children. There are the external aspects of life, but there are also interior matters."

Fumiko spoke about her life as we climbed a steeply rising, narrow trail that led further up into the mountains. She and the children had planned a picnic beside a stream, and she had brought along mixed sandwiches—ham, cucumber, and egg salad on white bread sliced into thin strips. She also carried cold rice balls wrapped in seaweed with a pickled cherry inside, cold tea, tangerines, and bananas. The trail was overgrown with crawling vines and tall grass, and on the way we passed along a dark, wet ledge where a waterfall tumbled from the ridge above us. Across from the stream, on top of a boulder, stood a small wooden shrine, where her mother-in-law used to pray for good fortune.

"Living with my mother-in-law," she said, "is the most unpleasant aspect of my life. Japanese customs are still feudal. Mothers-in-law have a lot of power. I can't do things the way I want to. I must respect the wishes of my husband's mother. I have learned to place my in-laws' needs above my own. I try not to get her angry, because she has a terrible temper. When I was younger, and my first child was just born, I couldn't do as much work as usual. And of course my mother-in-law couldn't do any work at all. Still, she scolded me. I learned to take it. I didn't let it bother me. But I have never said this to anybody else."

"Weren't there times when you couldn't bear up any longer?" I asked. "What did you do then?"

"I went to the toilet and wept." I looked up to see tears forming in the corners of her eyes.

The children were ahead of us, picking wild flowers and berries and gathering chestnuts and acorns from the ground. After lunch they went down to the stream to catch tadpoles in a handkerchief.

"I envy my brother's wife, because my mother is so kind to her." Her brother, whose wedding picture she showed me, was, like Fumiko, narrow-boned and handsome, with the slender face of a movie star. He had married the daughter of a banker, and lived in Tokyo, where he taught school. "Mother helped out when their child was born. She is very fond of my brother's wife. It has something to do with religion: my parents are strong believers in Buddhism. They belong to the True Pure Land sect. People with a strong Buddhist faith are kind to all others. They try not to block your path."

Fumiko's work in the fields went uninterrupted throughout her childbearing years. She worked till within a few hours of the delivery of her first child, giving birth at home with the help of a midwife in the middle of the night. Afterward, she did all her chores with the baby on her back. In the third or fourth year of her marriage, she lost part of a finger in an accident in the fields: she had not been accustomed to using the thresher. But she managed to write and even sew despite the handicap.

On our way home, we walked through the fields where Fumiko worked alone ten hours every day during the growing season. "It's quite a job," she said. The fields were scattered: first, a narrow patch of vegetables about ten feet by fifteen feet; next, three small rice paddies; and then, running up the side of the mountain, three terraced paddies. Down on the level ground, in front of her house, were three larger paddies, the only ones suitable for machine cultivation.

"Until three years ago," Fumiko said, "I didn't have any money of my own. Before that time, all my earnings from farming went to my father-in-law, who doled out an allowance to his wife and my husband. I had to ask my mother-in-law for money to buy even the smallest item, like milk for the children. She would examine the purchase, ask how much it cost, and take the change. When I visited my parents at New Year's time and Obon, they would give me some money to spend on the children or myself, but I was careful not to let my husband's mother know, because she would get angry. Three years ago, my father-in-law retired from the family business and my husband became president. He is finally able to draw a salary from the company. I get money from him. Also, I can now keep the money I earn in December at the open market in town, where I sell the rice, beans, and peas I grow."

After we reached home, Fumiko began folding the straw mats on which the rice was spread to dry. She had risen at five-thirty that morning, as she did every morning, and while I was still sleeping, she had loaded twenty-pound sacks of rice onto a wheelbarrow, pushed them from the storage shed to the front of the house, unrolled the mats, and poured the kernels of rice on them. "You must be tired," she said smiling. "Why don't you rest now?" She had a lovely smile, but I noted for the first time that the entire top row of front teeth were false and set into artificial gums that were fastened in her mouth with a metal clamp.

What troubled her most was that she lacked free time. "Once I had certain goals I wanted to achieve, but somehow with each year my efforts slackened." She wanted to read more, to study. And she wanted to sew and knit. But she had so little time to spare that she even neglected housework, devoting all her energies to farming. She did not mind the work; she even liked it, and she was eager to learn more about it. "If you read books and study, you can improve your crop. It would be interesting to learn about new kinds of seeds and fertilizers, comparing the various kinds to see if you can produce more." She only wished she did not have to farm *all* the time. A few years before, she had tried taking a correspondence course in mathematics. She studied after ten-thirty in the evening, when the rest of her work was finished. One night while studying, she fell asleep and her homework assignment fell onto the coals under the *kotatsu* and burned. She still had all her other assignments, and she showed me how her grades had steadily improved until finally she had received a perfect score. Sometimes she envied the men who worked in factories, because at five o'clock they were finished for the day, and their evenings were free, whereas she had no free time and no vacations.

The farm season began in April, when Fumiko ploughed the fields and spread chicken manure. Early in May she sowed seeds in nursery beds and a few weeks later, after the fields were harrowed and irrigated, she transplanted the seedlings. Throughout the summer she worked in the flooded paddies, spraying insecticide and weedkiller, carried in tanks on her back. She also took turns with other neighbors cleaning the ponds and tending to the irrigation of the paddies, making sure the water remained at precisely the right level. In September she began preparing for the autumn harvest. By October she was in the paddies reaping, and she spent the whole of November threshing and drying the rice. In December she harvested the beans and peas and sold them at the market. The New Year's holiday—three days of rest—was her sole opportunity to visit her parents, who lived about one hour away by car.

Yet she worked at a leisurely pace. It took her over thirty minutes to wrap a wedding gift, assisted by her mother-in-law, who grunted suggestions from the sidelines, and her husband, who addressed the greeting card. Her gestures and sweet, thin voice never lost that unhurried quality that had made her seem aristocratic when I first met her.

Fumiko spoke very little about her husband. She saw him infrequently, since he preferred to take his evening meal with his parents in their wing of the house, and joined his wife and children later in the evening. (His mother had begun cooking her own meals, because she and her husband were missing a lot of teeth and preferred "soft food.") Fumiko's husband was an indulgent father who cheerfully put up with his daughters' loud chatter and their endless games of cards. Gathered around the *kotatsu*, the grownups talked to me above the sounds of the television and the children's hilarity. The three daughters, aged eight, thirteen, and fifteen, were usually joined by cousins ranging in age from six to sixteen, and although the adults muttered "We can't hear each other," it was apparent that they were willing to tolerate the gaiety, and their mother's "Be quiet" was said in a low voice that was barely audible above the din.

Fumiko's mother-in-law also came to sit with us after dinner. Earlier, she had called to Fumiko from the bath house, "The water isn't hot enough. Please burn some more wood." The bath house, a few feet from the main house, was an unpainted wood structure the size of a small room. Squatting outside, Fumiko reached into the space under the bath house to feed wood into the heater. Within, a round iron tub set in stone held the bath water and the bather. "Come scrub my back," she called to her daughter-in-law.

Joining us at the *kotatsu*, the old woman wore a gray kimono and a gray apron over it, and her gray hair was pulled back in a bun. Her face was dark, almost brown, and her skin was slightly mottled. "Foreigners all look alike," she said suddenly, staring at me with a mixture of suspicion and friendliness on her face. "Are there go-betweens in your country or do Americans marry for love?"

Her grandchildren chimed in, saying their grandmother had had a love marriage, but the old woman claimed she could not remember. Pressed further, she lowered her face and said, "I'm embarrassed." To marry for love in her day had suggested licentiousness. Many women of her generation had married men chosen for them by go-betweens, and they saw their husband for the first time on their wedding day. If they knew each other before marriage and if they had approved of the match arranged for them, they found it difficult to reply when asked whether theirs had been a traditional marriage or a love match;

the meaning of the word love was vague, and many women replied the way the old woman did, or they said, "Ask my husband."

Fumiko's mother-in-law had known her husband for two or three years before they were married. After completing her schooling at the age of fifteen, she had acquired an American-made sewing machine and learned to use it. She became a sewing teacher, and gave lessons to her future husband's sisters at their home. That was almost fifty years ago, in the 1920's. Her early childbearing years corresponded to the period of militarism in Japan preceding the Second World War. In those days, she recalled, the average family had twelve children. "We were urged to bear children for the nation. School classes were canceled at the peak of the farm season so that children could help out in the fields. There was no time for children to study. And discipline began at an early age, by the time a child was three. Today, children do not do farm work, except on National Culture Day, November 3rd, when schools close for a day and the whole family ritually works in the fields. Nowadays, children are spoiled in their early years, and disciplined later on."

Throughout our conversation, Fumiko sat quietly sewing, though occasionally she interjected a word or two to explain to me in unaccented Japanese what her mother-in-law had just said. She seemed to enjoy playing the role of my guide and interpreter. It was an extension of the role she played in her children's education. Fumiko, and indeed her children too, had a familiarity with foreign culture that the other family members lacked. During my harvest-time visit, the girls' father commented to me that "it must be spring now in your country," and his younger brother asked if Saõ Paulo was in the United States.

Fumiko had read in translation a surprising number of American classics, including Louisa May Alcott's *Little Women* and some of Hemingway's novels, as well as books on race problems in America. In fact, she kept a record of all books read by her and the children and put red dots next to the "really good ones." Among them were *Crime and Punishment*, *Hamlet*, Andersen's *Fairy Tales*, *Aesop's Fables*, and *Gone with the Wind*. Apt quotations and favorite lines from each book were carefully copied down. She also made quizzes as a game to test her daughters' knowledge: Which Japanese novelist recently won the Nobel Prize for literature? Which of the following was born in such-and-such prefecture? What is the name of the heroine in a Maupaussant short story?

Fumiko's efforts to educate her daughters in her values underscored her high expectations for them: she bought a tape recorder and English-language conversation cassettes, and arranged for an older cousin to teach them the piano. She now had free rein to spend generously on them, and to give them what she herself had been denied. Her daughters, unhampered by the need to learn farming, were expected simply to do well in school, and Fumiko took complete, personal charge of overseeing their progress.

Fumiko never spoke of education in terms of the advantages it might give her children professionally. What she emphasized was learning for learning's sake and the cultivation of the individual. Once when we were alone, she casually remarked that it was "just as well the Japanese lost the war," because defeat and the American reforms during the Occupation period had brought democracy and, with it, equality and enfranchisement for women. "If Japan had won, militarism would have continued, and individuals could not live for themselves. They would be asked to keep sacrificing for the country."

On the second day of my visit, Fumiko took me to the local primary school to see an exhibit of old farm tools, and from there we went to the bookstore in town to look for histories of the area. Once we were in town, away from the rest of the family, it was easier to talk, and I suggested stopping at a coffee shop, one of the few places where privacy is possible in the rural areas. Sipping coffee in a corner booth of the dimly lit shop, I mentioned the conversation on marriage I had had the same morning with one of her neighbors, a young woman who had recently returned from Osaka, where she had been working for several years at a printing press. When she turned twenty-five, both her employer and her parents had expected her to quit work and marry; she had returned home to have her family arrange a marriage. When I asked the young woman what was the most important thing to look for in a marriage, she had immediately replied, the man's family background. "If you think too much about marriage, you'll never get married," the young woman had added, somewhat puzzled by my probing questions.

The account of my conversation elicited from Fumiko a monologue on her own unhappy life. She had wanted more from life, she said, especially a better education. "My husband is seven years older than I," she continued. "I felt as though I were marrying my grandfather. His way of thinking is different from mine. He doesn't like books and he doesn't have many talents or hobbies. With him it's only work. We don't have interesting conversations. . . . But he is well liked by others and has many friends. And so I endured, I became resigned." I looked up to see, once again, tears welling from her eyes.

After we left the coffee shop, as if to make up for her loss of control she threw herself into food shopping. She would not allow me to pay for anything, and tried to choose food that I would like. "Do you like cake? How about butter? I know—pears!" She took three, each one costing about twenty-five cents. When we left the store, she insisted on carrying my book as well as her groceries, and when we boarded the bus, she paid my fare. She seemed determined to make up for burdening me with her innermost thoughts, even though I was honored that she had trusted me. I did not know how to say this, however, without causing her further embarrassment, so instead I could only allow myself to be the recipient of her generosity. My departure from the hamlet the next morning was accompanied by a lavish showering of gifts: a sewing box, a Japanese-style jacket, a pair of slippers, a pencil and eraser (from the children) in the shape of a doll, and a haiku poem written by my hostess at midnight after the rest of us had gone to sleep.

I saw Fumiko several times after that weekend. The extravagant generosity she had shown me on the day of my departure from her home proved to be characteristic of her behavior in general. It was a generosity that went far beyond the simple kindnesses and courtesies of other farm women, and above all it came to symbolize for me her almost studied gentility.

At a New Year's gathering when she met Haruko and her family for the first time, she slipped the children a thousand-yen note (about three dollars). When she later learned that Haruko was sick in bed, she sent her the equivalent of six dollars. The receipt of a gift, however small, called for reciprocity, and within four months she and Haruko had exchanged five such gifts. After getting the last one, Haruko became exasperated. "There's no end to this," she said.

At other times too Fumiko was quick to hand out money for gifts. When I bought a present for one of her daughters, who was hospitalized with appendicitis, she immediately handed money to me. Punctilious to the point of compulsion, she displayed a generosity that, while not improper, was perhaps old-fashioned and even tedious to other, more modern-minded women of her generation. Residents of Bessho, in fact, had agreed a few years earlier not to give or expect to receive return gifts as reciprocity for hospital presents. They had found that hospitalized patients risked relapses if they tried to return all the presents they had received.

I could not tell whether Fumiko's generosity was a form of *noblesse oblige* or simply represented the pleasure of someone who had waited thirty-six years to acquire spending power and was delighting in her newly won liberty. Perhaps it was a mixture of both.

As I came to know more of the ways of farm women, I was increasingly struck by her separateness. In Haruko's view, she was simply old-fashioned. "Her behavior is more prevalent among sixty-year-olds," Haruko said. "My mother-in-law is like her."

I showed Haruko a sample of Fumiko's handwriting, one of the haiku she had written to commemorate my visit. The poem itself was not expert; it lacked a reference to the season of the year. The calligraphy, however, was, in Haruko's favorite words of praise, "first-rate." Fumiko was talented and educated, she was saying.

"She's read many books, too," I told Haruko. "She's got a record of all the books she's read since junior high school."

"Well, that's certainly not typical for a farm woman."

"And she studied the tea ceremony for two years. Yet she kept saying that much as she wanted to educate herself, to study more, to develop her hobbies, and that sort of thing, she had no time. So I sympathized with her. 'That's a shame,' I told her. 'I'm awfully sorry.'"

Haruko laughed.

"What should I have said?"

"In that situation, Japanese say, 'Oh no, you are really very talented.' You write well, *neh*" (here she drew out the Japanese version of "don't you" or "you see" so that it sounded like a whinny), "and you studied the tea ceremony, *ne-e-eh*, whereas I can't do anything."

"At the time, I believed she really did lack an education, but later I got to wondering."

"She was sincere, she meant it," Haruko assured me. "You see, the Japanese are modest to a fault. There are times when you don't know how they really feel, what they really think. Their mouths and their stomachs aren't the same. You say what you really think. And I do, too. My mouth and my stomach are in accord. I'm simple. It has to do with one's basic character. I was born that way. But there are some people—mind you, not everybody—who don't say what they really think. They tell me, for example, that my chrysanthemums are pretty. Even if the flowers are shriveled and wormy, they say, 'My, how pretty.' But, if they confess that their children aren't good students, and you agree with them and say, 'That's right, your kids are dumb,' they get angry."

If Haruko observed only the minimum of good form, Fumiko was a study in social decorum. Only six years apart in age, the two were a generation apart in style.

IO

Social Life and Social Organizations

IN THE SECOND WEEK of December, Shō-ichi and his business partners threw their annual *bōnenkai*, or year-end party, and for the first
time invited their wives. Like New Year's parties in American offices,
such social gatherings serve to reaffirm ties of loyalty and cooperation, reward workers, and mend rifts. The party was held in a private
room of the Matsuya, an inn boasting the best food in Uwa; and in
addition to a variety of seafood dishes, a generous amount of *sake* was
served.

As soon as we arrived, we learned that some of the wives had at
the last minute decided not to come. Several of the men, as well as
Haruko, took turns on the phone trying to persuade them to change
their minds, and finally they appeared, only to drift to one part of the
room, leaving the uninhibited Haruko and the professional hostess
hired for the evening to chat with the men.

The hostess was clearly experienced in her work, which called for
establishing a mood of conviviality. Dressed in a kimono, she entertained the guests with a brief folk dance, gracefully executing delicate
movements of hands and feet. Afterward, drinking, smoking, and
talking with an air of knowledgeability—all the things proper wives
were expected not to do—she also proved expert at managing the
more intoxicated men in the group.

Before long, Shō-ichi, flushed with *sake*, fell asleep on the floor.
Meanwhile, the other men succeeded in getting themselves and the
old cleaning lady drunk, and the president of the company even

danced a fox-trot with her. (She looked pained and confused.) Later, the president held my hand, while one of the other men asked me to teach him the western style of dancing.

The wives, meanwhile, stayed by themselves. One, the mother of four children, had been up since five in the morning. Because her husband was employed full-time at the Agricultural Cooperative, she did all the farming on her own. She sat in silence, looking stolid and exhausted, and probably wanted nothing more than to go to bed. The women did not like the roisterousness of men's parties, they said; they would rather talk with each other. But they agreed that drinking was one of the few ways men could relax. What did women do to relax? They answered almost in unison that they went shopping.

For the most part, couples hesitate to go out together and have few occasions to do so. Few people can articulate the reason for this division of the sexes, except to say it is "embarrassing" to appear in public with one's spouse. Men also claim it is boring and costly to go out with their wives. And women claim it is "tedious" to go out with their husbands. "He'll berate her in front of others," one man acknowledged. "Besides, all men ever do is drink *sake*." One woman, unenthusiastic about traveling with her husband, said, "He'll only tell me to fetch his cigarettes or bring over a suitcase." "If my husband comes along with me on a trip," said an older woman in her sixties, "he has me fetching his baggage and getting him tea on the train." Even if a man and wife want to travel together, however, they usually cannot, because one must stay behind to tend to farm chores.

Of course farm couples spend more time together than urban couples in either Japan or the United States—they work side by side in the fields—and this may be one additional reason why husbands disdain going out with their wives, and wives do not expect to be entertained by their husbands. Haruko, though she was sometimes disappointed when Shō-ichi went to a party without her, seemed to feel that the behavior of Japanese couples nevertheless had its advantages. "No wonder so many people get divorced in the United States," she said, learning that American social life is based primarily on couples. "No wonder they feel constricted. It is a strain always being with the same person."

The Utsunomiyas socialized more as a couple than most others in their area. They had a small circle of close friends whom they invited to their home to enjoy informal evenings of conversation laced with laughter and singing. These friends tended to be townspeople, educators, and Socialist party members. Two of their regular callers were town women, who visited without their husbands. Occasionally the Utsunomiyas also entertained Shō-ichi's young protégés—farmers who, like Shō-ichi, had been abroad—together with their wives, but the young women looked uncomfortable, remained silent, and, like the wives at the *bōnenkai*, congregated at one end of the room. Only Haruko seemed capable of closing the traditional gap between the sexes, talking freely with men and women alike.

Both custom and preference have kept alive the social segregation of husband and wife in rural Japan. Even youngsters are sensitive to the propriety of this custom. When Haruko announced that she would accompany her husband to hear me give my talk to her son's sixth-grade class, Hisashi was mortified. Haruko finally agreed to drive to the school with another mother, entering the classroom through the rear door while Shō-ichi and I used another door at the front of the room. We arranged to leave separately and picked her up at a street corner in town.

Sexual segregation is less rigid before marriage. For one thing, young people have opportunities to socialize with members of the opposite sex in school and in hamlet-based youth organizations. Even so, it is commonly believed that compatible marriage partners are best chosen by one's parents in consultation with respected, experienced go-betweens, and modified versions of the arranged marriage are still popular among parents, as well as among young people themselves. In remote farm regions, moreover, where unmarried men and women are scarce, young people have no choice but to rely on go-betweens.

Although rural men and women work together in paddies and on ditch-digging teams, they remain separated in most other public situations. Women do not attend hamlet council meetings, they do not participate in hamlet festival activities except as spectators, and they rarely go to the various parties and celebrations their husbands are invited to by friends and fellow workers. At funerals in the hamlet, women serve as caterers, donning white smocklike aprons over dark slacks and preparing food for the family of the deceased, while their husbands, dressed in western suits, white shirts, and ties, formally represent their household as mourners.

One of the few legitimate occasions for married couples to go out together is the family gathering, on New Year's Day, Obon, and festival days celebrating the autumn harvest. They also appear together at funerals and memorial services for close relatives. All these occasions require elaborate feasts of traditional foods, and all of them except the funerals are catered entirely by female relatives. As a result, they are not always welcomed by farm women, who must spend many extra hours in the kitchen. The ancestral home is the site of most family get-togethers, and since Shō-ichi was the first son and family heir, the job of receiving his relatives and cooking for them fell largely to Haruko. Even Obāsan was relieved to learn that only her daughters would be visiting her at New Year's. "It gets very hectic with all those people around."

Family gatherings are informal affairs whose principal activity is eating and drinking. There is no waiting for other guests or for the host and hostess to begin: guests start eating as soon as the food is offered to them, from large platters laid out hours before, and they eat on and off throughout the day. The hostess may grab nibbles of food in the kitchen, join the company briefly in the guest room, and then fly back to the kitchen again. Even in the informal atmosphere of the family party, however, women guests, some still wearing their white aprons after helping the hostess, congregate at the end of the room, closer to the kitchen, and men sit at the other end, closer to the alcove, where the guest-of-honor customarily sits.

Other opportunities for meeting people were provided by a variety of societies and associations. Men and women of all ages pursued hobbies and mutual interests in local clubs. Haruko and Shō-ichi, who lived near the thriving town of Unomachi, had several to choose from, including the haiku society. Haruko spent every available moment, her brow furrowed, laboriously composing the traditional seventeen-syllable verses required of society members; Shō-ichi showed

Haruko (front row, second from left) and maternal relatives dressed for cooking and catering at a memorial service for Haruko's grandmother.

greater flair and facility, and he ranked higher in the society's rating system. Shō-ichi also belonged to Bessho's Chinese song club, and Haruko went to flower-arranging classes.

Married women typically socialized with other married women. They tended to be segregated by hamlet and by age group in a variety of organizations geared to meeting their particular needs and interests. A new bride might belong to the Young Wives Club. Like other women between the ages of about thirty and fifty, Haruko attended meetings of both the Women's Guild of the Agricultural Cooperative and the Parent-Teacher Association. Women in their mid-fifties, who had "received" a daughter-in-law, might join the Mothers-in-law Club, and the older women could join the Widows Club or the Old People's Club, which was open to men and women alike but was attended primarily by women. Though younger men have no structured organizations like these, they sometimes form small private groups; Shō-ichi, for example, belonged to the Twenty-six Club, a group of about a dozen local officials and businessmen who met for dinner and conversation on the twenty-sixth of each month.

Membership in women's organizations provides not only fellowship but instruction in practical home and farm matters. Members also enjoy opportunities for travel and sightseeing with other women. If women cannot rely on male company, they can, thanks to the women's associations, participate in organized trips that are relatively inexpensive, enjoyable, and—precisely because their menfolk are not present—relaxing. Groups of women sharing one room in an inn stay up late to sing, talk, and perform traditional Japanese folk dances, which, appropriately enough, do not require partners.

The strongest of the women's groups is the Women's Guild, which was established in 1949 as part of the nationwide Agricultural Cooperative. Its avowed purpose is "to elevate the position of farm women" and "to borrow the strength of women" for Cooperative causes. The guild is organized hierarchically, beginning with chapters at the hamlet level and continuing with larger groupings at the township, county, prefectural, and national levels. Elections for leadership positions are held at every level, and membership fees and activities are determined by the leadership of the prefectural level—salaried women serving in the capital city of each prefecture. Membership in the Women's Guild is virtually obligatory for rural women. In 1973, women from about half of the five million farm households in Japan belonged to the guild, and at least one woman from each member household is expected to attend meetings and take her turn serving on the executive board of the local branch.

In the early years of its existence, the guild gave farm women a rare opportunity to leave the confines of their homes and socialize with other farm women. It also offered valuable instruction in home economics, arranging classes in practical matters such as cooking, nutrition, and seed selection. For example, women learned how much soap to put into their new washing machines and how to keep fat from spoiling. The guild also arranged for reduced prices on the purchase of women's work clothes, underwear, cosmetics, and sanitary napkins.

Although the organization continues to perform these services, assisting women in their roles as farmers and housewives, busy farm women found the many rounds of classes, meetings, and related administrative tasks time-consuming and burdensome, especially since membership duties usually fall on women who are also engaged in farming, childcare, and part-time jobs. The teacher at the "Mrs. Kitchen" cooking classes introduced complicated recipes with the injunction, "If you find cooking bothersome, you can't be a good cook." The class was virtually compulsory: women were expected to take off time from their wage-paying jobs to attend. "The Women's Guild is the root of our troubles," said one farm woman.

Insofar as it can draw upon considerable social pressure to oblige women to participate, the Women's Guild resembles not so much a voluntary association as a prewar organization based on communal solidarity. The annual election of the president and vice-president of Bessho's guild was illuminating. Since the vice-president in one year automatically serves as president the following year, the election was pro forma. When the results were announced, however, the newly elected president, a woman of about thirty who had three small children and a part-time job as a clerk, burst into tears, protesting that she was too busy to serve and that her husband, a primary school teacher, would be angry. Other guild members reminded her that, as the current vice-president, she should do what was expected of her. When the weeping woman begged to be released from her obligations, a compromise was proposed: a delegation of members would go to her husband to gain permission for his wife to serve. The following week, at the next level of elections, the most vociferous critic of the weeping president-elect was herself elected to office and stubbornly refused to serve, pleading ill health.

One aim of Women's Guild leaders was to encourage farm women to communicate with each other. As one guild leader explained, "In the past you talked with your neighbors while working in the paddies. You would take a break and sit down on a rock, and while nursing your baby you would talk about your problems and air your feelings. These days everyone is employed outside the hamlet. There are times when you don't even know that your neighbor is home sick in bed. You still help each other in a formal way, but you don't freely share feelings with each other." Many women were indeed troubled by their lack of communication with their neighbors, and they would surely have welcomed the opportunity to share their feelings and opinions freely and honestly with others.

Yet the guild, with its obligatory and structured meetings, did not lend itself to such openness. For confidantes, Haruko relied on her several town friends and on the four or five women who attended flower-arrangement classes with her. Women at guild meetings were usually silent. The salaried leader of the Uwa guild exercised herself with all the professional exuberance of a schoolteacher in front of a slow class (formerly she had in fact been a schoolteacher), resorting to pep talks, moralistic lectures, and even group songs to inspire the women's active participation.

As I later came to realize, the women were so burdened with other responsibilities, they could take no interest in formal group activities. Sleeping only six or seven hours a night, their days fragmented by the numerous tasks they were expected to perform on the farm and at their wage-paying jobs, they naturally tended to doze off when the guild budget was read to them. The letters written by farm women to the salaried leader of the Uwa Women's Guild reflect the real center of their interests and the way these have changed. In the past, their letters had mainly inquired about how to prepare traditional Japanese foods like pickled vegetables, whereas recently they had begun to show the women's interest in handling their money wisely to cope with inflation, in raising and educating their children (and especially establishing rapport with them), and in finding outside work.

Farm women's concerns do not extend to politics, and in any case, by the terms of its charter the Women's Guild is a nonpartisan organization. But the ruling Liberal-Democratic party (LDP) does exercise a subtle influence on guild women. The holding of guild meetings in hamlet social halls and in the Agricultural Cooperative building puts women in direct contact with officials who support LDP candidates. There are usually three or four men in semi-official capacities—Agricultural Cooperative functionaries, Buddhist priests, or directors of the social hall—whose salaries come either from the Cooperative or from the government and who set themselves paternalistically over the local women's guild in their area. Whenever I went to talk with a women's group, I was always first introduced to these local male officials, who in turn introduced me to the waiting women and then remained to moderate the discussion. "It would be better if the men were not present," I whispered to my hostess as I was escorted into a room to interview members of the Women's Guild of a fishing village. "This is the way it's done," she muttered in reply.

On one occasion, the head of the Uwa branch of the Agricultural Cooperative entered the room at the beginning of the monthly women's meeting, sat down in the guest-of-honor's seat, and gave a brief speech in which he asked the women to sign a petition supporting a local LDP candidate for the upcoming election. Haruko was furious. Everyone knew her husband was a local leader in the Socialist party and was a possible candidate for the very same office. And yet, she said, describing the scene that evening to Shō-ichi, everybody in the room had "bowed to the great man." She had sat in silence: what could she have said?

Hearing her account, Shō-ichi himself got angry. "If you thought you were right, you should have spoken up."

"But how could I?" she retorted. "Even if the other women had agreed with me, they would never have said so openly. I'm just a farm woman," she added, and then, looking significantly in my direction, "I'm not a professor."

"What about quitting the group?" I asked.

"I can't. I promised I would serve on the executive board this year. Besides, the others would part company with me." Even her close friends, she felt, would drift away. Three women in Bessho had for one reason or another left the guild. One left because the meetings were gossipy. Another refused to serve on the executive board, and a third had a falling out with some of the other members. Although they appeared cheerful enough, Haruko suspected that they felt isolated and lonely.

Besides, there were several advantages to membership. The group took an annual trip, the meetings gave women a place to talk to each other, and, finally, the guild was educational. On the negative side, Haruko had to admit that the meetings were frequently "trivial," that service on the board was time-consuming, and that, of course, the LDP applied a certain amount of pressure to support its candidates.

Haruko was also upset about several other incidents that had occurred during the day's meeting. For one thing, many men from the Cooperative had attended the pre-lunch meeting and had talked about a lot of "uninteresting" things. Haruko did not want to hear about the "future of farming"; she wanted to learn about more immediate concerns—children, cooking, the wise use of money, and "rational household practices." When she said as much to the head of the Uwa branch of the guild over the phone that evening, the woman, a salaried employee of the Cooperative, instead of agreeing with her, had said something about the need "to endure—to put up with it," and also called on Haruko's sense of "public duty."

Much as she upheld the humanitarian goals of the Socialist party and despised the bowing and scraping of Women's Guild members, Haruko also opposed her husband's idealism and railed against the awkward position in which it had placed her. "It is hopeless to try to change these people," she said. "Why do farmers support a predominantly capitalist party anyhow? Why can't they see they would be better off with the Socialist party?" In a torrent of words, she answered her own questions. Some people resented the Socialist party for being the party of the workers, whose strikes raised prices and hurt farmers. More importantly, the LDP was in effect the principal guarantor of jobs and promotion in the area. Schoolteachers jeopardized their chances of promotion if they opposed the party, and Agricultural Cooperative workers could lose their jobs, or be transferred to a post in the hinterlands that would force them to live apart from their families or commute long distances. Haruko ticked off the names of all the job-holders in the area around Uwa who were beholden to the LDP: they included post office workers, town hall clerks, employees of the Agricultural Cooperative, and schoolteachers. Loyalty was rewarded, disloyalty was punished. It was as simple as that. "My husband was president of the PTA for four years and served in the town council for another twelve years," Haruko said. "He successfully led the land reform program, even though local LDP officials had opposed it and others had said only the LDP could pull it off. Usually such a record of service is rewarded with an official citation from the prefecture, but what did my husband get? *Hiya-meshi*—a raw deal." (Literally, cold, boiled rice.) "Well, such things sting."

At one Women's Guild meeting, the male head of the local branch of the Agricultural Cooperative gave a talk entitled "What the Women's Guild Should Be." He spoke of the need to find ways of handling the future, a popular theme at that time. His topic was an appropriate one for an audience of farmers, who in a general way were uneasy about the current inflationary prices and were particularly concerned about the potential effects of the 1974 oil embargo; the possibility of "hard times" was a frequently voiced concern.

The speaker's ideas seemed woefully anachronistic. He spoke of going back to one's roots, and many of his suggestions smacked of traditional Confucian moralism, which, if followed, would demand even more of already hard-pressed farm women. Haruko, however, who was usually so practical and independent-minded, listened respectfully as the speaker exhorted women to greater frugality, enjoining them to make their own clothes and to use water sparingly. He also urged them to abandon the practice of working outside the home and to concentrate on economies within the home instead. He even suggested that they work more in the paddies.

"Would you go back to burning wood?" I asked Haruko afterward. The old-fashioned, paternalistic, and above all else, long speech had put me in an argumentative frame of mind. "Are you willing to give up your washing machine?"

Haruko replied that although she herself was willing to rely more on her own labor power, women more accustomed to labor-saving devices might not be able to abandon them. And, she added, she would try to use less money.

"But you don't seem extravagant as it is," I persisted. "Where would you economize?"

"Toilet paper."

"Toilet paper?"

"People used to use newspaper. And I could save on food, too. We eat better than most other people around here."

"But if you economize and make your own clothes and heat the bath with wood, your life will be dull and, since you won't be working at a wage-paying job, you still won't have any money!"

"That's right," Haruko agreed, suddenly reversing herself. "And then there's the school fees—"

"And you told me you love to shop for clothes."

In the evening, as if to underscore the contradiction between her rational commitment to the traditional virtues of frugality and self-sufficiency and her emotional attachment to modern tastes and consumerism, Haruko applied one of her many face creams. This one, given the English name Pack, claimed to whiten the skin and remove wrinkles. Once applied, it hardens on the face like a mud pack and it peels off like dead skin: "I can't laugh," Haruko warned, grotesquely masked in the white, puttylike substance.

Face cream and western-style clothing for herself, a high school education for the children, and gasoline for the farm machinery all required cash, and Haruko's earning power helped make them affordable. It was true that all were examples of the consumerism decried in the guild speaker's talk, but they also represented a consumerism that the Agricultural Cooperative and the Women's Guild had themselves in part made possible and had encouraged: displays of kitchen appliances and even of gemstones were exhibited at the local cooperative, and clothes and cosmetics were offered at a discount through the Women's Guild. But I pressed Haruko no further on the subject. She aspired, like other farm women, to the material comforts of the bourgeoisie; and even if she were willing to use newsprint for toilet paper, only dire circumstances could persuade her to abandon her newly won feminine frills, not to mention her newly acquired economic prerogatives.

11

Sex and Drinking

BOTH HARUKO and her husband believed that sex was the basis of marriage; without it, a couple could not stay together. Quoting a popular saying, "Not even a dog is tricked by a couple fighting," they explained that angry couples will eventually make up in bed. Popular wisdom also pronounces on the frequency of sex after marriage, which, at least among Shō-ichi's male acquaintances, follows a fixed formula based on a multiple of nine. Couples in their forties, for example, typically have sex on the average of once every five days: four (for their fourth decade of life) multiplied by nine equals thirty and six, or, in thirty days, six times.

An active sex life is hardly fostered, however, by the sleeping arrangements in a Japanese house, which by virtue of its small size forces certain kinds of human relations on its residents. With five or six people living in three rooms, privacy is impossible. Doors slide open without warning; one cannot knock on paper, and to say "May I come in?" each time one seeks passage through one room to another, is a luxury few busy farmers can afford. One can well imagine the plight of the farm woman who, when she was first married, lived with her in-laws and her husband's two younger sisters in three rooms, one of which was devoted to silkworm cultivation. The young couple slept in the living room, through which everyone else in the family walked to get to the toilet.

Until recently it was common for parents to sleep with their children until they were as old as ten or twelve. The practice called for each parent to sleep with one child. Two mattresses were lined up alongside each other, and the children slept between the parents. Older children might sleep alongside the grandmother in the adjoining room.

Younger couples, if they could afford to, gave their children separate beds, and bunk beds were popular as space-savers. One couple in the hamlet had their three small children sleep in a bunk bed while they slept alongside on mattresses on the floor of their tiny room. A small measure of privacy was created by curtains drawn around the bed. Haruko and Shō-ichi had given their daughter a bedroom of her own when she was thirteen, three years earlier, and at the same time they gave Hisashi a small room and a separate bed. Such arrangements were becoming increasingly common among families who had the space to spare.

The trend toward separate bedrooms seemed to be related, not to the parents' sexual needs, but to the emphasis on their children's education. Children were getting not only their own beds and their own rooms, but also desks, lamps, and small bookcases to encourage good study habits. The accommodations did not necessarily meet with the approval of all education leaders. An article in the local PTA bulletin decried the weakening of family ties caused, it said, by the new custom of separate bedrooms.

Even among couples who could afford to give their children separate bedrooms, sexual relations required a great deal of discretion. Though the children might properly sleep alongside their parents, they were not supposed to know that their parents slept with each other, and propriety demanded that the Japanese wife roll up the bedding each morning and place it in a closet; it was considered especially indiscreet to leave out a double mattress covered with a single large quilt. Haruko and Shō-ichi departed from convention when they bought a western-style bed (actually a sofa that folded out into a double bed) and left it open during the day.

Explicit instruction in sex was largely unavailable to farm women until recent decades. Forty years ago, they married men they had never seen before and tried to follow their mothers' last-minute instructions to do whatever their husbands demanded of them. Two of

Haruko's friends had heard that in the old days the go-between waited outside the newlyweds' bedroom, listening at the door until the sounds inside confirmed that the marriage had been consummated, and then returned to the girl's family to report the good news. Stories still circulated of innocent brides fleeing in shock to their parents' house after the first night, complaining that their husbands had been rude to them.

Only in the past decade or so have women's magazines, found on newsstands and in the local library in town, provided detailed instruction in the art of love. The January 1974 issue of Women's Club (*Fujin kurabu*) contained a special illustrated feature entitled "A Calendar for Sexual Stimulation" that organized for women a month's worth of daily, systematic exercises for becoming an exciting partner. The illustrations themselves were chaste: a man and woman, dressed in leotards, their bodies never touching, posed in various love positions with the detachment of two physical education teachers demonstrating calisthenics. The text, however, left nothing to the imagination.

On the first day, the woman was advised to shower and then massage her body with cream or oil. On the second she should admire herself in the mirror after her bath. The third day found the trainee practicing her kissing techniques, assisted by drawings of heart-shaped mouths, arrows, and instructions explaining how to pucker up, move the mouth up and down, and so on. By the fourth day, the woman was ready to stick out her tongue and move it from left to right in preparation for the following day's goal, which was to learn how to use her mouth in the art of making love. For practice, said the guide, use a banana.

This step-by-step way of teaching sexual relations is characteristic of Japanese teaching methods in general. The instructor imparts confidence not so much in himself or in his pupil as in the method or the ritual, which, when scrupulously followed, eases the passage through potentially stressful situations. Articles preparing the bride for her honeymoon night are thus as detailed and systematic as those explaining the principles of flower arrangement or the proper way to cut vegetables.

Young Lady (*Yangu redii*) magazine's one hundred steps to ensure marital felicity advised the new wife in everything from getting her teeth straightened (step 66) to bringing along a bath towel on the honeymoon night in order to protect the hotel sheets (step 78). The young bride was reminded to close her eyes at the first kiss and let her husband take the first bath. She was also directed to lay out her husband's clothes after he entered the bath room, join him in the tub if he asked her two or three times, and jump out ahead of him to spread the bath towel she had brought along.

The honeymoon itself is a new custom in rural Japan; at least until the end of the Second World War, wedding festivities lasted three days and on the fourth, the couple returned to farming. When asked if she had taken a wedding trip, a woman in her sixties replied jokingly, "Yes, I went to the mountains." She meant that she had gone to work in the terraced rice paddies.

For information on contraception and on pre-natal and infant care, farm women in the Young Wives Club can draw on the services of a public health nurse. Family planning is the woman's responsibility in Japan, and since the oral contraceptive and the diaphragm are unpopular, most couples rely on condoms, which women purchase in the town drugstore. (In larger cities, condoms are dispensed from street vending machines or sold by door-to-door saleswomen.) One couple in Bessho reported using the rhythm method, and at least one man had had a vasectomy. Since the end of the war, abortion has also been a legitimate method of population control: special abortion clinics are accessible to farm women, who in 1974 paid a fee of about seventy dollars, perhaps a tenth of their earnings for the year.

Residents of Bessho and nearby hamlets that ring the bustling town of Unomachi also had ready access to pornographic magazines in the bookstores and coffee shops, though few had the leisure time for such diversions. It is more likely that at least once in their lifetimes they would have visited a museum of erotica in the nearby city of Uwajima. There, on the grounds of a Shintō temple, is the Dekoboko Museum (the Chinese characters for the name graphically suggest sexual intercourse). A Shintō priest sells admission tickets and mementos of the museum's collection of erotic art, pornography, and masturbation equipment from all over the world. Groups of men and women, usually middle-aged or older, regularly tour the museum, delighted by its contents. Even puritanical Obāsan remarked, with a slight smile, that she and her sister had visited the museum the year before.

The displays of erotica and pornography in the Dekoboko Museum present sex as a mutually satisfying, natural act, recalling the origins of the Shintō religion in the worship of fertility. There are photographs of elephants mating, pictures of loving couples in playful poses, and phallic symbols dating back to archaeological times. In contrast, pornographic magazines, sold at the store where children bought their school supplies, depicted sexual relations primarily in terms of sadomasochism. A typical issue of *SM* showed women tied up with heavy ropes across their breasts, or hanging upside down, or on their knees. "To excite," proclaimed the cover. Such scenes were almost always drawn in cartoon form, giving free rein to the fantasies of the viewers, who were frequently uniformed school boys, standing shoulder to shoulder in front of the store's magazine racks. Only once did I see a picture of a woman who seemed to be enjoying sex.

The subject of sex was not taboo in the village. Haruko herself tolerated sexual banter among the male farmers and laborers with whom she worked, saying sympathetically that it was the only form of entertainment available to them. She did not much care for the banter, but if one worked with the men, she said, one could not "put on aristocratic airs." Besides, she added, the man who did most of the joking had been working in the fields and ditches for the last twenty years; at night, when he came home, he ate dinner and went straight to sleep. He had no outside entertainment. If he talked "obscenities" it was because he was "looking for stimulation." Others could read books or magazines; he could only shoot off his mouth.

But sex, like everything else in Japanese life, was deemed to have its proper place. Haruko vehemently opposed sex before marriage. It was "wrong" and "dirty," she would declare with an air of finality. Haruko's view was the conventional one held by others of her generation and her parents' generation. This is not to say that premarital chastity has always been strictly enforced in the Japanese countryside. Indeed, numerous local customs not only allowed but positively encouraged young people to have sex before marriage. All-night trysts in the village dormitory, the custom of *yobai*—whereby a young man sneaked into a young girl's room at night—and even forms of trial marriage were familiar customs in parts of rural Japan until at least the end of the 1920's.* But the prevailing twentieth-century attitude toward premarital sex has been a conservative one.

Sexual mores seemed to be in a state of flux, however, especially among young men and women, many of whom chose their own marriage partners or worked in the cities before marriage—enjoying new wage-earning opportunities that made them increasingly independent of their families and their families' value systems—or traveled as agricultural trainees to the United States, where they absorbed American sexual mores. The standards of young people like these were perhaps a mixture of the new and the conventional. For example, young men of Shō-ichi's acquaintance felt that it was permissible for an unmarried couple to sleep together, but only if they were prepared to marry.

Changing attitudes toward sex and toward the modern woman's role in general were a topic of sufficient interest to draw busloads of farm women to a public lecture on the subject in Yawatahama. The speaker, Tomoko Inukai, was the author of a book called *Sabotage Housework* as well as various writings on American customs, and her talk was entitled "Goodbye, Housewife." An audience of about fifteen hundred women, including Haruko and members of the local PTA and Women's Guild, gathered to hear her. Inukai's argument centered on the theme of changes in sexual and moral standards in western countries. (She illustrated the theme early on with a slide of Marilyn Monroe dressed in a t-shirt and shorts.) The topic was of more than passing concern to the many kimono-clad farm women in the audience, whose future well-being was closely tied to the morals

*See, for example, John Embree, *Suye Mura, a Japanese Village* (Chicago, 1939), pp. 193–95, and Ōmachi Tokuzō, *Kōnin no minzokugaku* (Ethnography of marriage) (Tokyo, 1968), pp. 236–42.

of the younger generation, and who were aware that social trends in the West were frequently transmitted to Japan: a lecture on contemporary European and American life-styles might conceivably describe their own futures.

Inukai noted that the life-styles of men and women of all ages were changing. Men, for example, might dress like women, and vice versa. Young people had begun to live together in co-ed dorms. (Here Haruko gasped.) And children were now being given an early sex education. (A photograph from a sex education book was projected, showing a man and woman in bed; parents showed pictures like these to their children, Inukai explained, to teach them that sex was natural.) Women's liberation was flourishing in the United States, Inukai continued, and sex roles were being reversed: there were female jet pilots and male mama-sans. (Laughter from the audience viewing a slide of a man holding a baby in the nursery.)

Citing examples such as these, Inukai enjoined her audience to free themselves from their traditional roles as housewives and mothers. The fixed values of the past were giving way to new, rapidly changing values, and women, she said, should learn to think like individuals, to decide on their own what they wanted to do with their free time, what they wanted to wear, and how they wished to conduct their sex lives.

Haruko found the talk "very interesting," but she thought it would be difficult to follow a completely individualistic path as long as "feudal" elements remained in Japanese society. And though she was inclined to be "modern" and individualistic in certain of her own family relationships—for instance, in her cool, not altogether filial behavior toward her father and mother-in-law, and her desire to live apart from her son in her old age—she drew the line at sexual license outside of marriage. In this stand she certainly was not alone.

When I asked Shō-ichi about men's views on sex, he replied as follows. In the love life of Japanese men, he said, an order of preference exists: the least attainable woman is the most desirable. He listed, in descending order of seductiveness, another man's wife, a household maid, a mistress, a geisha, and last as well as least, one's own wife.

Despite this fanciful hierarchy of desires, however, Shō-ichi, like other men and women I met in the community, expressed firm adherence to a norm of marital fidelity.

This attitude struck me as odd at first, because husbands and wives rarely socialized together. Shō-ichi frequently attended parties on his own, leaving Haruko at home. Once a year, he also took a brief vacation trip by car with three or four male friends. Hostesses at the restaurant or inn catering to the men served their meals for them at the table in their room, and they also stayed to joke with them and pour their beer or *sake*. There was usually a great deal of flirting and jokes with sexual innuendo. Yet the men's fidelity was not doubted.

Sometimes I attended a party with Shō-ichi or took day trips with him in the car, to meet new people or just to keep him company or to see the surrounding countryside. Haruko, however, showed no signs of jealousy or suspicion. Men at the parties teased Shō-ichi about me, or said jokingly to me, "Now if you ever have any trouble with men, just call on me; I'm sure Shō-ichi will help you too"; but the very fact that they joked in this way suggested the seriousness of the subject.

"My wife knows she can trust me," one man told me. "She has no doubts about me." The man regularly went to cabarets to drink and joke with young bar hostesses. But he never went further than that. He did not need to bother telling his wife where he was or when he would return; he knew his wife would not worry about him. Nor did he think of taking his wife with him. He preferred going alone, in his free time, to be liberated, as he put it, from job and family responsibilities. But this sense of liberation was, in effect, an illusion, which the obliging young hostesses and the *sake* helped create.

Knowing the ways of Japanese husbands and wives, I was surprised by Haruko's reaction one night when I offered to accompany Shō-ichi to the mountains on his night watch over the pig farm. He had returned drunk and tired from one of a round of end-of-the-year parties, and was asleep at the *kotatsu*. When Haruko tried to wake him, reminding him he had to leave soon, he mumbled something about being too tired, and asked if I wanted to go along. I couldn't tell whether he was joking, so I did not reply, but I was worried about his ability to make the short but dangerous ride alone over the icy mountain roads. Haruko said he should have asked one of his partners to take the watch that night. She then asked their son if he wanted to accompany Shō-ichi, but Hisashi refused with an abrupt no. Finally, moved by Haruko's nervous fretting, I reluctantly volunteered to go.

"You can't!" Haruko cried. Later, after she had managed to wake up her husband and send him, alone and groggy, on his way, she came into my room with a serious look on her face, to tell me that in Japan one simply did not do such a thing. Her husband had been joking. My very mention of the idea of spending the night with her husband had shocked her. She barely maintained her composure. I explained that I had not known whether her husband had been joking or asking a favor of me and, since it seemed legitimate to accompany him everywhere else—whereas it would not be in the United States—I truly had not known what was expected of me and had been concerned only for her husband's safety. She understood, but nevertheless was shaken, not, I suspected, because she mistrusted either her husband or me, but because she feared the gossip of others.

Not long after, Shō-ichi phoned to say he had arrived safely and Haruko relayed to him our conversation. Shō-ichi thought the whole incident was funny and continued to tease his wife. "He said he'd like you to join him," she reported.

Bessho owned to one case of adultery in its recent history. It had occurred several decades ago, but Haruko still vividly remembered the details. The woman had been widowed at the age of nineteen and left with one child. Her family had arranged for her to remarry, taking the new husband into their household as an adoptive son-in-law. The marriage did not work out well, however, and she began seeing a man who was married and had children of his own. A friend of his in Bessho helped arrange their liaisons. Meanwhile, the woman gave birth to a child by her second husband. After many stormy scenes, the adopted husband was returned to his parents' home, and the couple was divorced. The tempestuous widow-divorcée then prevailed upon her lover to divorce his wife, and eventually she married him. Since the woman's new in-laws refused to accept her children into the family, they were sent to her second husband's parents to be raised.

For all their notoriety, the adulterers were not judged harshly either by fate or by the other residents of Bessho. Their children by previous marriages and their own children intermarried with Bessho families. Moreover, once married, the couple settled down to a life of hard work, and the family fortune doubled. The wife earned a reputation as a capable worker and was considered, along with Haruko, the fastest rice transplanter in Bessho. The family's prestige was measured by the funeral of the man's mother: thirty-six paper floral wreaths—an unprecedented number, sent by friends, relatives, and business acquaintances—stood decorating the front of their home. Still married to her third husband and apparently happily so, Bessho's adulteress was now a sprightly woman in her mid-sixties.

The forty-five households in Bessho included several divorced persons, though the prevailing attitude, among the married women in the hamlet at any rate, was that divorce was not a legitimate solution to marital problems. One elderly man had married at least seven times; another man had had four wives in succession. Among the divorced women was one whose husband had left her and their child for another woman. She had remained in Bessho, living in the hamlet's Buddhist temple, where she performed perfunctory caretaker duties in return for her board. There was one retarded, unmarried mother, and recently, one girl, who was rumored to have been living with her boyfriend and to be pregnant by him, was hastily married off to him. All these cases were violations of acceptable social behavior; but only the adulterous affair of several decades ago was considered truly a scandal.

Whereas sexual attitudes were by western standards fairly rigid, attitudes toward heavy drinking were positively relaxed. Even the most extreme drunken behavior was cause not so much for moral outrage as for annoyance, if indeed it was commented on at all.

The village drunk, a forty-year-old carpenter who looked sixty-five, commuted by railroad three hours each day to work in Matsuyama, frequently arriving home late and in a drunken stupor. His wife had the reputation of being a shrew who yelled at him and told him not to bother coming home if he was drunk. As a result, he came to the Utsunomiyas' house instead, sliding open the doors of the entryway at midnight and muttering, "Excuse, excuse," over and over again as he swayed from one side of the entryway to the other. He would then struggle up the step leading to the living room and plop down at the *kotatsu*. Rather than put up with his antics, Haruko would flee to the bedroom, sit behind the door, and take out her knitting and listen. Shō-ichi and I were left to fend for ourselves.

On one such occasion, having entered in his customary manner, the carpenter began by babbling for a few minutes and then, pausing only to steal a cigarette from Shō-ichi's pack, he proceeded to show me picture postcards of the shipbuilding yard where he worked. Shortly, as he poured himself a glass of whiskey, he promised to leave if I would sing a song. I did. Then he sang a song. Shō-ichi became impatient. He told the drunk man quietly but firmly to leave.

The drunk staggered to his feet and then, looking like an actor out of a thirties screen comedy, he opened the wrong door and headed toward the sleeping quarters. Halfway to my bedroom, he realized his mistake, turned around, and stepped back into the living room. Sliding open the doors, he climbed down into the entryway, tripped over the shoe closet, and stumbled out the front door.

As soon as he left, Haruko flew out.

"First-rate," she said to me, excitedly. "He was fine tonight. That's because you were here. Ordinarily he shouts at me, loses his temper, and stays until one or two o'clock."

The next morning, at about ten, the carpenter reeled down the road clutching his lunch box, still swaying and unsteady on his feet. His wife would not let him stay home to nurse his hangover.

A few days later, the carpenter tried to kill himself by drinking fertilizer. He was distraught over his wife's nagging: the night before, she had told him, "You'd be better off dead." She found him in the bath and saved him by forcing him to vomit. Later in the week, Yōko overheard her berating him.

Perhaps because of the strained family life in the carpenter's household, his two children were among the few students in the area who did not go on to high school. His daughter failed her entrance examination, and his son decided to become a carpenter instead of entering high school.

Haruko's sympathies were almost entirely with the carpenter. She felt his wife was not taking enough care of him. "She won't let him drink in the house. She should keep whiskey in the house and offer it to him; then at least he'd be safe, go to sleep, and not bother others."

Haruko's tendency to blame the drunk carpenter's wife for his drinking problem typified the reaction of most rural women to drunk men. The inebriated were to be humored and cared for. Since drinking was the principal diversion of male farmers, and since they became tottering, babbling drunks, after only a short time at the bottle, tolerating inebriated men was a part of the farm woman's routine.

Women tried to avoid being with men when they were drunk and themselves refused to drink when the men tried to force *sake* on them; but when all else failed, they laughed good-naturedly, and played along with the men. At one party, attended mainly by junior high school teachers, the few women who were present hovered around the edge of the festivities, sat in a separate room, and left early. One female guest, heading for the door, narrowly avoided a stumbling drunk, somehow fending him off and exiting smoothly with a smile on her face. The host's seventeen-year-old daughter also behaved in a decorous, quietly amused, and tolerant way, even when one man took her hand and tried to sit on her lap. "He won't remember anything tomorrow," she said, sagely, her knees tightly clasped together and her hands, once freed, resting gracefully in her lap.

"Men drink when they are tense," Haruko explained. "Drinking is their way of relaxing. One should just go along with them." Haruko truly practiced what she preached, as one unforgettable incident confirmed. It was graduation day, and the two vice-presidents of the PTA, together with two primary school teachers, dropped by unexpectedly at five in the evening. They chose our house to celebrate the end of the school term, because Shō-ichi had served four consecutive terms as head of the PTA, and had that day given a brief address to the graduating class, one of whose members was his own son.

Haruko hurriedly threw some snack food on the table. She had just returned from her daily visit to the hospital for an injection to help her over her head injury. Shō-ichi, honored by the visit, urged his guests to drink and before long, he got quietly, happily, and sleepily drunk. One of the primary school teachers had arrived completely intoxicated, drunk out of his senses, and began making amorous advances toward Yōko. He put his arm around her neck and pulled her closer, while Yōko squirmed, trying to smile bravely as everybody laughed. She finally freed herself and hurried into the kitchen, with the schoolteacher in pursuit. Haruko was preparing coffee and only laughed as the man tried to hug her daughter, who was by now visibly upset. Finally, Yōko slipped away, got on her bicycle, and escaped into town.

Shortly afterward, Haruko and one of the PTA vice-presidents, a woman, were frantically trying to pull the drunk man out of the kitchen, where he was preparing to urinate on the stone floor, and push him out of the house, where it is considered proper for men to relieve themselves. The man had already unzipped his fly, but did not have his shoes on. The PTA lady flew to the entryway, grabbed a pair of shoes, and hurried back to put them on the staggering schoolteacher. The two women managed to push him outside, using the sort of motherly admonitions commonly administered to a three-year-old, all very politely: "Sensei, you mustn't go out without your shoes," and "Sensei, no, no, be careful," and even "Sensei, no! You mustn't pee in here!"

Meanwhile, the men sat drinking and attempting to talk above the din. One of the other women closed the door to the living room so that they wouldn't be disturbed. Soon the schoolteacher staggered back inside the house and, standing in front of us, zipped his fly before falling down on the floor. When he raised himself up again, the PTA lady kept a watchful eye over him, making sure he did not hurt himself—again acting like a mother supervising an active toddler. When he stuck his fingers in the dish of pickles, she removed the dish.

When he tottered over the ledge of the living room, she grabbed hold of the back of his shirt. When he clattered into the kitchen and toppled over a bucket of water, she rushed to remove his wet socks.

Any concern expressed by the women was for the man's safety. They never lost their respectful, cajoling tone: "Sensei, please rest. You'll hurt yourself." But the Sensei, his eyes downcast as though he were blind, and his full, red bottom lip sagging, continued his antics uncomprehendingly.

"He's always very gentle," said the PTA lady.

"He's weak when it comes to drinking," said Shō-ichi, gently. Finally, Shō-ichi tried to get him to lie down on the floor next to him, patted his backside, and even lay alongside him as though the two were lovers. But the teacher kept popping up again, like a *daruma* doll, asking to shake my hand.

At last, he stumbled into the kitchen, again tripped over the bucket of water, spilling it all over the floor, and, backing away, stuck his elbow through a pane of glass, shattering it.

Shō-ichi smiled dreamily. "He can't hold his whiskey," he said.

"We can ask the school janitor to fix it," offered the other teacher.

"Oh, no, don't tell anyone about this. Don't tell Sensei about it," said Haruko. She quickly swept up the broken glass.

At this point, the other guests suggested that the man be taken home. While Haruko was telephoning for a taxi, however, he disappeared, wearing my slippers and leaving behind his jacket and shoes. The other guests left (it was now seven-thirty), Shō-ichi fell asleep, and Haruko and I went out with a flashlight, searching in vain for the schoolteacher.

"Maybe you should call home," I suggested.

"No, it would be too embarrassing for them."

"Couldn't you pretend you had a matter to discuss with him?"

Haruko phoned. He was home. Haruko told his wife she would bring his shoes and jacket to the school. No trouble at all. Sorry to bother you.

After she hung up, she turned to me and said, "He's usually such a quiet man."

The following day, the teacher stopped by to inquire whether he had been to our house the night before. He was carrying one of my two slippers. He remembered nothing of the previous night's revelry, but promised to look for my other slipper.

A few hours later, he returned with a new pair of slippers, a box of cakes, and a brief apology.

"He didn't see the broken window pane," Haruko sighed, relieved.

"What a dreadful man," said Yōko.

Whenever Shō-ichi went out for a night on the town with his friends and some bar hostesses, Haruko barely took notice, because these were public and legitimate forms of male entertainment. What drove her into a frenzy, however, were occasions when Shō-ichi arrived home either too late or too drunk (or both) to carry out his family, business, or social responsibilities. One night, for example, Shō-ichi returned home from a party pleasantly drunk and glowing.

"I was kissed by two women," he announced, proudly.

"Who were they?" I asked.

"Two hostesses. They said, 'Mr. Utsunomiya, please kiss us.' So I did." He puckered his lips and made a smacking sound to imitate the sound of his kisses. He was elated.

Haruko smiled perfunctorily and then, her mind absorbed in more serious matters, changed the subject, asking, "Daddy, what should we do about feeding the pigs tomorrow? If you come home late from the birthday party—"

"Oh, I'm so thirsty."

Haruko got up to bring him a glass of water.

"Two women kissed me—"

"Daddy," Haruko repeated, with her familiar tone of anxious urgency, "what do you think?"

Shō-ichi said, "I'm sleepy."

Suddenly Haruko became agitated, remembering that it was her husband's turn to spend the night at the pig farm. "Daddy, you can't go out tonight! Get somebody else!"

"Wake me in thirty minutes," Shō-ichi muttered.

"I tried to work in the potato patch today," Haruko said, changing the subject, "but by evening, my head began to hurt again."

Ignoring her, Shō-ichi asked me, jokingly, whether I wanted to accompany him to the mountain pig farm.

"Yes, certainly," I replied, going along with the joke.

Haruko became agitated. "Say, 'I should go, but I'm busy,' " she instructed me. "You know, people don't always understand your sense of humor. Obāsan, for example—"

Shō-ichi leaned back on the floor, stretched out on his back, and laughed.

"Those poor women," I said, "making them kiss you."

"No, no. *They* asked *me* to kiss *them*."

"Oh."

"Daddy, cancel your commitment tonight. You can't go out."

Shō-ichi was already asleep on his back.

An hour later, asleep in my room, I was awakened by the sound of Haruko's panic-stricken voice crying, "Daddy, Daddy, wake up!" She was slapping his face. "What a mess! What should I do? He can't go out like this, in this downpour, in his condition. Are you all right, Daddy?"

Shō-ichi remained sound asleep.

"Go to bed," Haruko said to his sleeping form. "We'll get somebody else."

Shō-ichi groaned.

"We'll say you're sick. You have an upset stomach. If this had happened two hours earlier, it wouldn't be so bad, but at eleven o'clock at night—what should we do? Daddy, go to bed!"

Haruko finally roused him and he stumbled into bed. She telephoned one of his partners, who agreed to take his turn. In the middle of the night, Shō-ichi began vomiting and continued gagging and retching until noon. In the early afternoon, feeling a little better, he left alone for the birthday party. He and Haruko argued before he left, because she wanted him to take her along, but he refused. At the party, to be polite, he drank about two glasses of beer and returned at five in the evening to attend a wedding in Bessho. Haruko took over his chores and fed the pigs.

12

Yesterday, Today, and Tomorrow

WHEN I QUESTIONED HARUKO about the younger farm wives in Bessho, she bristled. She did not care for some of these women in their twenties, she said, and she downright disliked a few of them. "They don't have to farm, and they are better off financially than I was at their age. Their lives are much easier than mine has been and yet they complain." A few also put on airs, Haruko implied, referring to the standard Japanese spoken by one young woman, a nurse who had never farmed. Haruko made it clear that my sympathies should not go to spoiled young women whose lives had not been forged in hardship as hers had been. She identified with the older generation of women in their late fifties and sixties.

Women born in the early years of the twentieth century still carried vivid memories of stoking kitchen fires with wood they had gathered in the mountains, of drawing water from wells some distance from their houses, and of washing clothes in nearby streams—chopping holes through the ice in the winter. Women of Haruko's generation shared with these older women the wartime memories of malnutrition, of whole villages emptied of their able-bodied men, and of women's defense drills. All rural women born before the end of the war farmed, raised silkworms, made their own clothes, and, as they frequently say, endured.

The benefits of an improving standard of living in the countryside in the last two decades have been translated into labor-saving equipment for housework and modern machinery for farming. It is only the generation represented by Haruko's daughter, however, that has been freed entirely of farming and given a genuine opportunity to complete high school and, sometimes, college. Women of this generation, if they do agree to marry farmers, will probably not farm themselves. The greatest beneficiaries of increasing prosperity and agricultural mechanization are thus the successive generations of young people who are now receiving more schooling, better nutrition, and more material possessions.

Generational differences among farm women were apparent in their clothing. One young farmer's wife wore a mini-skirt, and for underclothes a western-style bra and panties; "my husband doesn't like me to wear layers of undershirts," she said. Women in her mother's and Haruko's generation wore a combination of western and Japanese clothing, reserving the Japanese style for formal occasions, and women in their sixties and older wore mainly the Japanese style: a kimono for working around the house and visiting, and baggy pantaloons for working in the fields. Such clothing preferences among farm women reflect more than the vagaries of fashion; they demonstrate the availability of western ready-made clothes and women's increasing participation in a widening money economy. Shopping —primarily for clothing—has become a favorite diversion of farm women; and for women of Haruko's generation, who in their youth rarely had money of their own, and wore only what they brought with them to their husbands' households or made for themselves, the experience is a new one. Trends in women's dress also signal the spread of western influences in general.

Changes are occurring in many areas of social life, affording young wives not only new material comforts but also a new status. One change actively promoted by the women themselves was the new trend in marriage ceremonies, and a drive to rationalize weddings had recently been organized in the Unomachi area by the Society for the Reform of Daily Life. In the old days—and as late as the nineteen-sixties in some areas—rural weddings were elaborate and costly affairs: three days were spent feasting at the groom's house and paying formal visits to the neighbors of the groom's family in order to introduce the bride into her new community. Nowadays, some couples chose shorter, simpler wedding celebrations lasting only one day, and took honeymoon trips afterward. The weddings were held on neutral ground—in the town social hall, for instance—and the bride's family shared forty percent of the costs.

Today's young people also have more say in the selection of their marriage partners, though many marriages in the countryside are still arranged by go-betweens—uncles, neighbors, or friends of the family. Women of their grandparents' generation recalled seeing their husband's face for the first time on their wedding day. One woman in her sixties, when asked if her marriage had been an arranged match, replied, "It was a forced match." Today couples date a few times before consenting to be wed.

The marriage of one young farm woman, Mrs. Shimizu, from the mountainous area of Nomura, was a mixture of both new and traditional elements. In 1975, at the age of twenty, she married a twenty-five-year-old carpenter whom she had been seeing for two years. Although theirs was a genuine love match, the family's next-door neighbors, a couple in their late thirties, were asked to serve as go-betweens, not only to legitimize the match but also to play the go-betweens' traditional role in overseeing the marriage ceremony itself, escorting the bride and supervising the ritual three rounds of toasts with *sake* that constitute the marriage ceremony.

The wedding was a modified traditional one: it lasted only one day. Since the groom was a *yōshi*, an adopted son-in-law who, in effect, was marrying into the bride's family, which lacked a male heir, custom called for the bride and groom to reverse roles, in the sense that he supplied the dowry and assumed her family name and she escorted him to her family's house, where her parents held the wedding.

Throughout her wedding day, the bride sat or stood or walked in silence, unsmiling, her head tilted forward at a forty-five degree angle—weighted down by a heavy and elaborate wig. Her face was completely transformed by white makeup applied early in the morning by a paid bridal consultant. In her red, brilliantly embroidered, rented bridal kimono she got in and out of cars, walked up and down steep mountain trails, and climbed in and out of houses for seven

Young farm woman (*above*), dressed in a mini-skirt, plays with her son, while her husband's eighty-year-old grandmother (*right*), with whom the couple live, prepares for work in traditional garb.

The newly married Mr. and Mrs. Shimizu pose for pictures on their wedding day, accompanied by their go-between.

hours of ceremonial greetings, ritual rounds of toasts, photography sessions, and exchanges of formalities, while the bridal consultant and go-betweens fussed over her, arranging the folds of her robe and adjusting the ivory comb in her wig. At last, the bride exchanged her robe for a lightweight kimono, removed her wig, and settled down with the wedding guests to a feast prepared by the bride's neighbors and served in her parents' house to relatives and close friends. The celebration, consisting of eating, drinking, singing and card playing, lasted until two in the morning.

The next day, the bride, looking once again like herself in a youthful red and pink kimono, drove off with the groom in his white fastback car to give final greetings to his mother. The groom, who had been dressed like a samurai for his wedding, was casually attired in black-and-white-checked slacks, a sports shirt, and a cardigan. On the following day, they attended his brother's wedding, and the day after that the two newly married couples left together on their honeymoon trip.

Upon their return, the young Shimizu couple settled in their own apartment in town, where they planned to live for one or two years before moving into her parents' house. The bride's father was seriously ill, and after his death the young husband would become household head.

Newlyweds today enjoy far greater independence than was available to earlier generations. Many young farm men and women still move into the households of their spouse's parents, but as the household income derived from farming becomes steadily smaller, the couple grows increasingly independent of the parents financially. In Bessho younger couples were asking for title to their parents' farm land or at least a share of it early in their married lives, instead of waiting until their father reached fifty or fifty-five and formally retired. Although the two generations continue to farm together, the son enjoys a farm income, in addition to his wages from outside work, separate from his parents' income. Legal claim to the land, and separate farm income, not only contribute to the economic independence of young couples but, indeed, also serve as an inducement for them to remain in the countryside.

Marital residence patterns are also changing. Although traditional obligations to live with and care for one's parents in their old age are still observed, young couples now seek privacy for themselves early on in their married lives. "Living together" with the old couple may mean working the land with them but no longer requires eating together and sleeping in adjacent rooms. Whenever space and money permit, young couples move into their own homes—usually one- or two-bedroom dwellings close to the main house, where they can set up separate housekeeping. When the older couple retire, and sometimes even before that, they typically exchange houses with the younger couple and their family, relinquishing the main house and moving into the smaller one.

An indication of the new social status of the young farm woman is her acquisition, earlier rather than later in her marriage, of the "rice scoop"—the power of the purse and the privilege of cooking the meals, dishing out the food, supervising the children's upbringing, and taking charge of the household. Stories told in village Japan describe women like Haruko's mother who deferred to a mother-in-law in all household matters until the older woman's death. As late as the nineteen-sixties it was not unusual for a woman to wait until she was forty and had been married for twenty years before she was allowed to cook for her husband and raise her children in her own way. Rural women say that today such cases are the exception.

To signify the change in the daughter-in-law's status, a new word has appeared in her vocabulary—*hatsugen-ken*, the right of expression. "I have the right to express myself," one woman said. "I can now argue with my mother-in-law or my husband." Under the old family system and prewar Confucian ideology, women hesitated to speak freely out of deference to their in-laws, in whose house they lived. And "right" was not a legitimate term. Since the Second World War, however, the new value system taught in the schools—which recognizes the concept of democratic rights—along with social and economic changes in the position of farm women, have helped establish *hatsugen-ken* as a common term of reference.

Among younger couples the rigid social separation of the sexes is slowly breaking down. "Married women ride in the car with their husbands, who carry the baby and the baggage," noted one woman in her sixties. "Younger couples show their feelings more freely. They hold hands in the street. They sleep in a separate room apart from their children." Her own marital relations were very different, and only recently have women of her generation begun going places with their spouses—to visit daughters in another city, to attend a meeting of the Old People's Club, or to attend a wedding. Even so, the woman continued, "I have nothing to say to my husband. I enjoy the company of my friends so much more."

Patterns of childbearing have also changed. Women born since the end of the war are likely to give birth to their first child in local maternity clinics or hospitals instead of at home with the help of midwives or "experienced women." Obāsan recalled giving birth to her first child with no assistance at all: "My stepmother had no experience bearing children, and my own mother was dead. When the first labor pains came, I said nothing, not knowing if they were serious and probably not wanting to complain. My husband went off to a sumo-wrestling match, and others were away from the house. Finally, I asked neighbors to call the midwife, but before she could arrive, I went into the toilet and, squatting on the floor, I gave birth to my first child and then passed out." Farm women gave birth either squatting or lying on the floor or, according to some sources, in a kneeling position. Modern medical assistance became available only in the late 1950's, but women whose childbearing years were in the 1930's and 1940's generally reported easy deliveries lasting only a few hours from the start of labor—one woman, born in 1900, said that her first child simply "popped out." Traditionally, farm women worked in the paddies until birth was only a few hours away, and they returned to work after thirty days, leaving their newborn in the care of their mothers-in-law. Today, however, many young farm wives do not farm at all, and they do not take wage-paying jobs until their children are of school age.

Farm women today have fewer children. During the 1930's and 1940's, large families were encouraged by the government and families with twelve children were awarded a prize, but since the end of the war, the legalization of abortion and the widespread use of contraceptive measures, together with numerous other factors, have resulted in a marked drop in the birthrate. Whereas it was once common for a farm family to have six children or more, today two or three is the norm.

The lower birthrate, coupled with the migration of young people to urban centers, has in turn led to a drastic decline in the population of the countryside. Furthermore, many farm men are frequently away from their households at work in the towns and cities. As a result, traditional attitudes toward the participation of women in the public and social life of the countryside are slowly being eroded. In Bessho, for example, women may now go in place of their absent husbands to the hamlet council meetings, which traditionally they were prohibited from attending. And in the township of Akehama, young girls have been given the privilege of carrying the portable shrine in the harvest festival, because there are no longer enough young boys in their early teens to serve as carriers.

An illustration of the changing way of life of both the farm family and the young farm wife is the case of the Uesugi family and their daughter-in-law, who were relatives and neighbors of the Utsunomiyas. The father and the mother of the household were in their sixties. Mr. Uesugi made his living buying and selling forest land, and Mrs. Uesugi worked with him to grow rice, tobacco, and grapes. Their eldest son and heir-apparent had gone to college, studied art, and renounced his claim to the family's land in favor of a job teaching art in a Tokyo high school. Their second son agreed to stay on the farm. After graduating from high school, he spent two years in the farming-training program in the United States, and in 1966, when he was twenty-six years old, his parents asked Shō-ichi, their nephew, to arrange a match for him.

Shō-ichi chose Yoshiko Hoki, the twenty-year-old daughter of another Bessho family. Her sister was married to Shō-ichi's brother. Yoshiko had just returned home after working for two years in an office in Osaka. She had enjoyed her work and had lived securely in the company dormitory, but homesickness caused her to give it up. Her parents had tried several other matches through another go-between before Shō-ichi arrived on the scene. The two young people went out on a few dates and then agreed to the marriage, which Yoshiko later described as neither a love marriage nor an arranged marriage, but something in between. Her parents found the match convenient because, having lived in the same hamlet as the groom's family for decades and being distantly related to them, they could forego the customary investigation into family background.

After their marriage, the young couple had lived with Mr. and Mrs. Uesugi for one year before moving into an attached wing containing three small rooms and a small kitchen. Their three children slept in bunk beds in their own room. Even after the couple had been married for nine years, and had established a separate household with separate finances and eating arrangements, Yoshiko's mother-in-law still hovered around their living quarters during the day, and when I arrived for an interview with Yoshiko, who had been primed earlier by Haruko to talk freely to me, her mother-in-law, probably more out of politeness than nosiness, joined us and stayed until I left.

Dressed in a red sweater and slacks, her hair professionally curled, Yoshiko seemed relaxed and unhurried. One of her children was in primary school, the other attended nursery, and the third romped around the room as we talked. Although Yoshiko did not do outside work, she helped out occasionally on the family farm, working with her husband and in-laws in the tobacco field and also bagging grapes.

Yoshiko said she raised her three children without any interference from her mother-in-law, and she also freely purchased daily necessities for them, herself, and the house, though she and her husband decided together on more expensive consumer purchases, and her husband made all the decisions related to farming. If Yoshiko had any complaints, it was that she rarely had conversations with her husband: they had nothing to talk about, she said, and she envied American women, "who go out with their husbands." Her social activities revolved around her work in the Bessho Women's Guild: having replaced her mother-in-law as the household's representative, she was serving a term as treasurer, and she also belonged to the Young Wives Club.

The life-style of young women like Mrs. Uesugi, though typical of a general trend toward increasing material comfort, early economic

independence, and freedom from grueling farm work, does not necessarily represent the lives of all young farm women in rural Japan
today. The fate of farm women depends in large part upon the local
economy, which in turn depends on geography and other factors.
Women in isolated villages lead harder, lonelier lives than those living close to urban areas like Unomachi, where social activities and job
opportunities abound. Rice plains are more prosperous than mountainous regions that can only cultivate rice on terraced slopes. It is
therefore impossible to talk about Japanese farm women as if they
represent a single entity; regional as well as age differences produce
a variety of life circumstances.

Even within Higashiuwa county, where I collected my data, there
were striking contrasts in the life-styles and economic circumstances
of farmers and their wives. The county is 200 square miles in area and
varied in terrain. In the four townships that constitute Higashiuwa
county, geography plays a critical role in defining economic opportunities. Akehama, squeezed between steeply rising mountains and
the sea, relies for its livelihood entirely on fishing and on the cultivation of *mikan*, introduced after the Second World War. Citriculture
requires year-round labor, leaving little time for side jobs; yet the income from *mikan* is barely adequate. Only a few miles inland, Uwa,
on a broad rice plain, has for many hundreds of years been a center
of transportation and administration in the county. Its residents can
take advantage of the commercial opportunities in Unomachi or can
commute by train from Unomachi to one of several important cities:
Uwajima, thirty minutes to the south, Yawatahama, thirty minutes
to the north, and Matsuyama, one and one-half hours to the northeast.

Farther inland, in the isolated, mountainous regions of Nomura
and Shirokawa, where farming is conducted in small, fragmented
paddies climbing steeply terraced slopes, incomes are inadequate to
support even a small family of four. Here the terrain will not allow
extensive machine cultivation; transporting the produce is slow and
costly; and few side-products other than mushrooms will grow during the harsh winter months. As a result, male household members
seek comparatively well-paying jobs in industrial centers on Honshū,

working on construction teams or in factories as *dekasegi-nin*—laborers who work away from home for six months or more.

The wives of these laborers—*dekasegi* widows, they call themselves—must for much of the year bear the burden not only of farm labor but also of farm management. They must make decisions about seed purchases and must prepare the tax returns. They must deal with Agricultural Cooperative officials or with village leaders—and in small, traditional communities, such responsibilities can cause great anguish for housewives unaccustomed to them. The strain of farming mainly on their own and of living with their in-laws without the support of their husbands creates special medical problems for them: the incidence of miscarriages, abortions, and gastrointestinal ailments is abnormally high among *dekasegi* wives.*

The future of farm women in this rugged region of terraced rice paddies is insecure. Few can make a living any longer. Inflation has absorbed their meager farm income and has driven their young men to live permanently in the cities. In one village the drop in population has forced the high school to close; the children must board in another village until they graduate, when they will probably be compelled to seek work elsewhere. The greatest concern of *dekasegi* wives is therefore that they will lack successors to inherit their farms. They would prefer to remain in the countryside and have their children live with them, but in their old age they will probably have to uproot themselves and move to the cities to join their sons' families. Meanwhile they wait out their time, isolated from the neighboring hamlets and isolated even from each other. By day they work the fields alone or they try to make ends meet by taking on small jobs sewing parts of dungarees or feeding mulberry leaves to silkworms, and at night they stay home in front of the television set rather than walk dark, twisting paths to a neighbor's house. In such economically depressed rural areas women have living standards ten or twenty years behind women from more prosperous farm regions.

At the opposite end of the social spectrum in rural Japan are women who neither farm nor work for wages. Some are married to

*See, for example, Watanabe Sakae and Haneda Shin, *Dekasegi rōdō to nōson seikatsu* (Dekasegi labor and rural life) (Tokyo, 1978).

farmers whose income from agriculture and other sources is adequate to support the family without their help. More typically, they are the wives of white collar workers—schoolteachers, postal clerks, or Agricultural Cooperative employees—and they live in towns surrounded by farm communities. In this study, they make only a brief appearance as Haruko's town friends, but although they are not farm women, they too are a part of rural Japan. Indeed, they remain significant in the life of the farming community because, as a leisure class, they embody the ideals and the life-style the working farm woman aspires to—the dream of being "just a housewife."

For the Japanese farm woman, the idea of women's liberation, if it means anything at all, means freedom from the economic uncertainties and physical drudgery of farming, more time to spend cooking, cleaning, and sewing, and the opportunity to help the children with their homework. The Japanese farm woman, in short, yearns for a strictly domestic role. When told that an increasing number of American women find domestic chores trivial and seek what they term meaningful work outside their homes, the farm woman responds with a mixture of puzzlement and annoyance. "Such complaints," said one woman bluntly, "are a luxury."

This difference in the aspirations of women from different cultures and classes underscores the need to place all social movements in both a cultural and a historical context: where you want to go depends on where you have been. Hard physical labor of the sort the Japanese woman has done in the fields with men for hundreds of years has not inspired in her the same enthusiasm for men's work that might excite daughters of the American suburbs. Nor does the farm woman dream of office work or a profession. She wants instead what she feels she has been cheated of: a chance to stay at home, where she can create a clean, leisurely, healthful environment for her family.

The housewife ideal is given expression in the many television shows and commercials promoting urban, middle-class values. It is further reinforced by the Women's Guild, which encourages women to learn new recipes, attend cooking classes, and scrupulously oversee the nutritional requirements of family members. With greater exposure to western society, farm women may also be acquiring their conception of the better life from overseas influences.

For the Japanese farm woman this bourgeois feminine ideal by no means connotes lack of self-reliance, or dependence on her husband. Farm women currently make important decisions affecting family members—decisions about the children's education, household purchases, and, in recent years, farm management. Not only do most of the farm women surveyed keep the wages they earn and spend them as they see fit, but a great many of them manage their husband's salary as well, doling out an allowance to him. If they do not rely on their husband's help in household affairs and childrearing, neither do they expect his interference. They are mistresses of the household and, as a consequence, their husbands are in many ways dependent upon them.

Whether it is repairing the stopped drain in the kitchen sink that is called for, or dragging out a dead pig from the sty, the farm woman learns early to rely on her own practical know-how and physical stamina; so too does the urban Japanese housewife. They have never been placed on a pedestal, never made to feel helpless. In the absence of a traditional code of chivalry toward women, Japan has produced women who, of necessity, have acquired a strong degree of practical and emotional self-reliance that colors the role of the housewife in Japanese society. It is a role that is respected and is viewed as a profession in itself. The aspirations of the farm woman must be understood against this cultural background.

Finally, the Japanese farm woman's aspirations for herself are in large part inseparable from her aspirations for her family. The basic social unit in Japan, and particularly in rural Japan, is the family, not the individual. A large percentage of rural marriages are still arranged by go-betweens, a marriage system that minimizes personal involvement and emphasizes family continuity. Japanese farm women very often understand the concept of improved status, not in terms of their position in society, but in terms of the family's position. Improving their family's economic prospects, achieving a higher living standard, ensuring a good education for their children, and similar concerns have a real bearing on their personal status.

The major problem with the housewife ideal, as far as the farm woman is concerned, is that it articulates a life-style that is ultimately inimical to farming. Middle-aged parents today sympathize with their offspring's feelings of alienation from the land and their attraction to urban life. Witnesses to the declining rural population and sensitive to their children's ambitions, they know that they may be creating a lonely future for themselves and a tenuous future for farming itself in Japan.

13

Departure

ON MY LAST NIGHT in Bessho, Haruko and Shō-ichi had a spat. It was a one-sided fight, and Shō-ichi received a vicious tongue-lashing. He had come home too late and too drunk to join the family for dinner—a special supper of my favorite foods. Haruko had spent the whole week helping me with all the last-minute details attendant upon my departure, and she was exhausted. She had helped me pack and mail my cartons. She had also composed on my behalf thank-you notes in Japanese, printing, addressing, and mailing them to fifty people. Some of the recipients, like the camera store man in town, had helped me in one way or another with my work, and others, like the head of the township, had had to be thanked for form's sake only. Haruko had also helped me order and deliver to the Bessho social hall fifty bowls inscribed with my name and the date of my departure as remembrance gifts to the residents of the hamlet, and she accompanied me around the town of Unomachi one afternoon to call on a few people she thought deserved to be thanked in person. One of these was the town librarian, whom we visited in the hospital, where he was recovering from an operation. In each case, she instructed me to present a small gift, like Japanese cakes, to show my gratitude.

During these hectic final days, Haruko had somehow found time to supply me with various bits and pieces of missing information I needed to round out my research on women in the hamlet and to settle our financial affairs. She had done all of this while taking turns with other family members spending the night at Uwajima hospital with her father, who was still convalescing after surgery.

Haruko had wanted our final days together to be harmonious; she wanted everything to be just so. But the strain was getting to her. Earlier in the week she had given two farewell parties, which she had planned, catered, and orchestrated entirely on her own. Singing a farewell song at one of the parties, she had burst out crying, and on this, our last day together, she had fallen asleep in the middle of a sentence. Rousing herself, she had sat up, written five haiku as remembrances, folded the laundry, and begun preparations for dinner.

Meanwhile, Shō-ichi had gone off to a party he felt he could not miss. He had invited me to accompany him, but I had declined. When he returned home at seven-thirty, instead of five as Haruko had asked him to, the family was in the middle of eating dinner and he was so drunk he could hardly stand up. "Do you know the scientific name of those flowers?" he suddenly said in English (which he hardly ever used with me), pointing to the bouquet picked earlier that day by our neighbors' children. Before I could answer, he pronounced the name in Latin and then murmured, "I wish you happy." Turning to Haruko, he said, still speaking in English, "Give me some tea." She stared blankly at him, not comprehending, and he stumbled into the bedroom and fell asleep. An hour later, he threw up. An hour after that, rousing himself from bed, he got dressed and pulled himself together long enough to sit with me and Haruko for our final evening of conversation. This was when Haruko blew up.

She was sitting in her *yukata*, a blue and white cotton robe, her hair wrapped in a net, her face shiny with cleansing cream. She spoke rapidly, in a low voice, her mouth twisted in a sneer.

"You're really something. You and your talk about doing good for others, for society. But when it comes to your own family—that you neglect. You neglect your children. You promised to be home by five o'clock. And on her last night—her dinner party, too."

He had no defense. He admitted he had wronged me. He tried to repeat one of our old jokes about divorcing his wife and marrying a younger woman. "In Japan, women are great" (*erai*), he jested.

But it no longer sounded funny.

He became angry when she continued deriding him and, half seriously, half jokingly, he shoved her forehead with the palm of his hand, saying, "Be quiet!"

But she seemed not to notice, and suddenly I felt frightened.

"Write this in your book," she said to me. "This is how Japanese men use their wives. It's been going on for a long time. It comes from feudal society. We're supposed to be servants. They don't do anything in the house."

Shō-ichi turned to me. "Men's work is outside the house. One is expected to go to these gatherings. They're not exactly parties. This one had to do with the Town Hall. And you can't turn down drinks when they're offered."

"Other men," countered Haruko, "do more for their families than you do. You're worse than anybody else. There were days when my children did not see their father's face. What do you think of that?"

I did not want to take sides. I could not take sides. I loved them both; but they were such different personalities with such conflicting needs. She wanted him at home at her beck and call, to run errands and occupy himself with all her concerns. He needed to get out in the world, to have a goal beyond the home. She wanted more money; he wanted to accomplish social and political reform. She wanted him to take her out; he found her company boring. His spirit, in order to survive, had to be free of her nightly chatter. But did she chatter because she had nobody else to talk to, and rarely had a chance to talk to him?

The moment had come for me to drop my air of detached objectivity. Aloofness seemed a mean conceit with people I cared for and might never see again. Yet I hardly felt equipped to play marriage counselor in Japan, and like Shō-ichi and Haruko, I was exhausted from the day's activities. I did have my own opinions of their relationship, their way of bringing up their children, their relations with Obāsan; I felt they spoiled their son and treated Obāsan cruelly at times, but out of some sense of professional discipline, which now seemed misplaced, I had always backed away from their sincere interest in hearing what I as an educated outsider, with a different perspective, thought about their lives. Now I felt I had been wrong to disappoint them.

"Part of the problem," I ventured, "is the nature of social life is Japan. As long as men and women are segregated socially, and social life is mixed in with business and political dealings, it is difficult to change some of your husband's habits. A man is expected to attend these parties, drink, and come home late. But Japanese mothers are also to blame for spoiling their sons. Your son grunts 'More rice' and you leap up to serve him. Or he merely bumps his empty rice bowl against your sleeve and you comply. In America, children are taught to say, 'May I please have some more.' "

"He's probably imitating me," Shō-ichi said, penitently.

"I'm jumping up and down during the entire meal," Haruko said, complaining for the first time about her kitchen routine.

But we were all too tired to continue talking. Our conversation touched on a conflict characteristic not only of Japanese society, but also of American society, European society—was this pull of the woman toward home and hearth and of the male toward politics and society a universal theme? Haruko symbolized for me the spirit of service and un-self-pitying sacrifice. Her enormous energy and practical skills, her common sense and her noisiness, or *gacha-gacha*, and her desire to protect only her family's interests, her nagging—all of these traits were pitted against her husband's gentle refinement, his larger vision, his selfish use of the women in his family, his drinking, his romanticism. She smothered, he neglected; she protected, he let be.

I left Bessho the following morning. Gifts were still pouring in. The Japanese love send-offs and are punctilious about reciprocating gifts and favors. Consequently, I was inundated with last-minute presents. Fumiko, the genteel farm woman, and her husband drove in to give me four handmade vests she had stayed up all night to finish; the elected head of Bessho presented me with a *yukata* from all the residents of the hamlet; the junior high school principal brought a small doll; the local cake store phoned to offer me a box of cakes;

and Shō-ichi's aunt, the elder Mrs. Uesugi, gave me a plaque on which she had written, with a writing brush, a farewell poem. In the days before my departure, other Unomachi shopkeepers had shown their appreciation of my business by bestowing small favors: the camera shop enlarged two pictures for free, and the beauty parlor shampooed and set my hair for $3.30 instead of the usual $5.00.

Although few people in Bessho had come to know me well, everybody observed the ritual of parting. Thus, when we left the house to go to the railroad station, our neighbors came out to wave goodbye. Obāsan said I was like a bride, and Haruko, taking her cue from that remark, kept up a running stream of instructions as our car pulled away. "Wave, wave!" she ordered. "Turn around and look out the back window of the car. Wave again!" And Shō-ichi, from the driver's seat, said it reminded him of the send-offs given to village boys when they went off to war. "If you were Japanese," he said, "they would all have cried 'Banzai!' "

Thirty people were waiting at the railroad station in Unomachi as we drove up to the curb. Among them were the junior high school principal; the local newspaperman snapping pictures; Haruko's brother, along with his wife and children; the two eight-year-old girls from Bessho who had jogged with me; a family of five from Akehama, whose home I had visited on several occasions; and several people I did not remember seeing before. Those who had not already presented me with gifts (and some who had) gave me small travel presents—rice crackers, chocolates, notes with personal words of farewell, and money. The newspaperman gave me a copy of a recent newspaper that had an article about me, and the post office clerk handed me two pieces of mail rescued from the following day's delivery.

Haruko had warned me that I would be expected to say a few words to the assembled crowd, now numbering over forty persons standing in front of the railroad station in a light drizzle. I delivered the brief speech I had prepared, thanking everyone, and especially Shō-ichi and Haruko, for their kindness.

Then we all poured onto the train platform. The rain added to the sense of sadness. The Japanese are sentimental about partings, and by this time even people I did not know were crying. I avoided standing next to Shō-ichi and Haruko for fear I would break down altogether, but Haruko grabbed my hand just as the train came into view. She was trying to smile, but she cried as she said, "Be well." Others, ritually correct, sent regards to my mother. Shō-ichi stood apart from Haruko and me, but before I boarded the train, we shook hands, neither one of us daring to look the other in the eye.

I boarded the train with Yōko, who was coming along with me to help carry the luggage, inflated with last-minute gifts, from the Matsuyama train station at the end of the line to the ferry. She told me to open my window for the final scene in the farewell ceremony as the station siren shrieked its one-minute warning. Members of the send-off party now pressed forward close to the edge of the platform and grasped my hands through the open window. As the train started to roll and then picked up speed, their fingers slipped away and their faces flashed past me one by one until the train tooted, left the station, turned the bend, and headed north.

Bessho Revisited

SEVEN YEARS PASSED before I returned to Bessho. In the interim, the Utsunomiyas and I had exchanged occasional photographs and gifts, and they had kept me informed of certain key events in their lives. I knew, for example, that Haruko's mother and father had died, and that Obāsan's health had deteriorated. Shō-ichi had also written to tell me that in February of 1977 government auditors had given official approval to the agricultural reforms he had pioneered, and that the five hamlets involved in the restructuring of the paddy fields had celebrated the completion of the project with a ceremony held in April of the same year.

It was nevertheless difficult to assess at a distance the ways in which the passage of time had affected the Utsunomiyas and other members of their rural community. Had the family prospered? What new kinds of work were Haruko and Shō-ichi doing? What changes had occurred in the lives of other farm women since the introduction of heavy farm machinery?

Although I was eager to see Haruko and Shō-ichi again and to learn the answers to these questions, the project that took me back to Japan in January of 1982 required research in Tokyo, and I decided to delay going to Bessho until early spring. Haruko and Shō-ichi, however, had other plans for me.

Five days after reaching Tokyo, I received a late evening telephone call from Bessho. Shō-ichi, his voice filled with excitement, announced that he had declared his candidacy for head of Uwa township, and before I could comprehend the full import of what he was saying, he added that he wanted me to make an appearance in Uwa in order to offer *iwai*, congratulations or formal greetings. I was certain I had heard him wrong until Haruko got on the line and in a surprisingly calm, refined tone of voice further explained that they were in the final days of hectic campaigning. "Can you possibly fly down in two days' time," she asked, "to give your official endorsement on the day before the election?"

Their scheme sounded preposterous. As a foreigner, how could I possibly participate in any way in a local election? Besides, I was completely unprepared to make the long trip on such short notice. But Haruko was insistent. She repeated that she had been working night and day on behalf of Shō-ichi's campaign and that they would greatly appreciate my joining them to give everybody, as she put it, a "last-minute spurt of energy."

I tried to explain, "I've just arrived in Tokyo and it's such a long trip—"

"Naturally we will pay for your plane ticket."

I assured her I was not concerned about the money but about the trip itself. And what was the weather like in Ehime, I asked.

"It's snowing," she replied, cheerfully. "But the airport is still open. We'll send somebody to meet your plane."

Shō-ichi took the phone again. "I hesitated for several days before calling you," he said, quietly. "I decided to run only about two weeks ago."

I still had not recovered from my initial surprise at Shō-ichi's request, and having exhausted my objections, I could not think what more to say, so we agreed that I should sleep on the matter. But already I knew that I should not refuse.

Two days later I was hauling a suitcase filled with winter clothes in and out of four different trains before reaching Haneda Airport. I would be staying in Bessho for a week, which would give me a few extra days to visit with Shō-ichi and Haruko once the election was over. After the ninety-minute flight west along the Inland Sea, I arrived in a snowstorm at Matsuyama, where two of Shō-ichi's friends were waiting to drive me along icy roads through the snow-covered mountains to Uwa.

During the two-hour car ride from the airport, my drivers briefed me on the election. It was an important race because Uwa is the second largest township in the prefecture, and the position of head of the township could very well serve as a springboard for election to the prefectural assembly or even to the governor's office. Shō-ichi had decided at the last minute to enter the race after numerous supporters had urged him to challenge the incumbent, a man who had served for seven years and had run unopposed in the last election. Critics of the incumbent accused him of giving jobs and business only to his friends and backers, and rumors circulated about vote-buying: it was said that he spent the equivalent of twenty-five dollars or more (or less —everybody gave a different figure) for each vote.

Shō-ichi's opponent was backed by many local political figures, including most of the twenty-five members of the town assembly and many notables in the conservative Liberal-Democratic party. In response, Shō-ichi had put together a coalition of backers representing both conservative and progressive groups. Having been a member of the Socialist party and, for three years, director of the Agricultural Cooperative, he had made many friends among laborers, intellectuals, Cooperative officials, farmers, and townspeople, and his support cut across traditional political groupings. Shō-ichi, who hoped to establish a middle-ground position that could break the traditional strength of the conservative party in the countryside, was part of a new wave of politicians whose potential had recently been demonstrated in Yawatahama, where the mayor had been elected with the backing of a similar coalition.

If the notion of my participating in a local campaign had at first struck me as bizarre, it now began to seem appealing, though in the back of my mind lurked the vaguely uncomfortable feeling that it was inappropriate for me, as a foreigner, to become involved in local Japanese politics. But that is not the way Shō-ichi and his supporters viewed it. My role was to be two-fold. As an American professor who had come especially to endorse Shō-ichi's candidacy, I would first of all "lift the mood" of the campaign workers. It was hoped that my appearance would give a last-minute boost to morale in Shō-ichi's camp. Second, I would enhance his reputation by giving living proof of his cosmopolitanism. As many people said, I would show that he had "a broad face." Other friends, including a doctor from another prefecture, had also come to speak on his behalf, the reasoning being that important friends are the measure of the man. But since the other side could also recruit distinguished Japanese supporters, I became Shō-ichi's unwitting trump card, or, as one excited campaign worker put it, "the flower of the campaign."

A local political campaign in Japan resembles a village festival. Campaigning for office is as much a matter of creating a festive air as of articulating political stands. To be sure, there were speeches, delivered earlier in the week, and there were slogans, such as Shō-ichi's promise to "build a clean township on a clean election." But neither incumbent nor challenger ran as the official candidate of any party, nor did either put forward a platform of specific issues. Ultimately the campaign boiled down to personalities rather than political ideologies. Both sides tried to gather around them legions of personal supporters and to demonstrate this support by having carloads of loyal followers accompany them and by otherwise maintaining a kind of exuberant momentum, like football players before the big game.

Shō-ichi's campaign headquarters was a small house in Unomachi directly across the street from the Town Hall, but the spiritual heart of his campaign was the social hall in Bessho, all of whose residents, with the exception of two men, supported him and were involved in one way or another in his election effort.* During the final week of the campaign, residents of Bessho gathered in the large meeting room on the second floor of the social hall to take their lunches and dinners, prepared by hamlet women in the kitchen on the ground floor.

When we arrived in Uwa, we made a brief stop in town to greet

*One of the two, Shō-ichi's brother's brother-in-law, was a member of the town assembly and therefore felt beholden to the incumbent. The other was a man whom Shō-ichi, when he was director of the Agricultural Cooperative, had required to pay rent on Cooperative-owned land he had been using free of charge.

workers at Shō-ichi's main headquarters, and then we drove directly to the social hall, where I received a tumultuous greeting from the more than eighty people completing their dinner there. My dramatic appearance in support of Shō-ichi's candidacy had, it seemed, elevated me to a heroic level. Afterward, I realized that everybody who walked through the door was warmly cheered.

It was at the social hall that I finally saw Haruko and Shō-ichi. I was sitting in the meeting room, food and drink heaped in front of me, when Shō-ichi, slightly intoxicated, crossed the room, fell on his knees beside me, and wrapped me in a bear hug. Haruko, looking tearful, disheveled, and exhausted, entered a few minutes later. Like her old self, and as if I had never left, she began issuing instructions to me in a conspiratorial tone. "Thank everybody you see for their hard work," she whispered. "Say 'You're doing a fine job' to the women downstairs in the kitchen. Don't forget! Tell them, 'Keep up the good work.'" As we left the social hall, she hissed, "Don't forget. Thank them all!" Haruko's chronic sense of urgency had in no way diminished.

Arriving home at about ten o'clock, we sat down at the *kotatsu* and, because we had so little time, without making any effort to catch up on each other's lives, we turned immediately to the business at hand: the following day's schedule. It was planned that I should ride with Shō-ichi and Haruko in the campaign truck and should give a short speech wherever we stopped along the way. At my insistence, Haruko supplied the text of my greetings: "I have come from America on behalf of Mr. Utsunomiya. Seven years ago, while living in his house, I thought he was a very fine man. He had the qualifications of a leader." (This last sentence was my own.) "People of Uwa township: elect Mr. Utsunomiya. Make him head of Uwa township!"

The following morning we left the house at nine o'clock. The rice plain, buried under several inches of snow and surrounded by mountains, looked like an alpine fairyland, but the narrow roads were slippery and the temperature was close to freezing. Wearing white rubber boots, two pairs of gloves, and as many clothes as I could fit under my coat, I climbed up into the cab of a pickup truck that was equipped with a microphone and loudspeakers, and for the next

eight hours I rode the campaign trail. Haruko, Shō-ichi, and two supporters riding in the open back of the truck took turns blasting the
township with their appeals for support. The noise of the loudspeakers was deafening as they blared the entreaties across the rice plain:
"It's Utsunomiya Shō-ichi, Utsunomiya Shō-ichi! Help us build a
clean township and clean politics. I beg of you, I entreat you, help us,
help us, elect Utsunomiya Shō-ichi. This is the last time we will come
around. Help us, help us elect Utsunomiya Shō-ichi. Utsunomiya
Shō-ichi to the last, please, please. . . ." When Haruko took the microphone, she added that she was Utsunomiya Shō-ichi's wife. Her
voice sounded frantic, desperate, hysterical. By mid-afternoon, she
was hoarse.

We visited forty-eight of the fifty hamlets that make up Uwa township. (The other two, the incumbent's present and former places of
residence, were squarely behind him.) Shō-ichi's supporters escorted
us in their cars, behind us and in front of us, wearing white gloves
and waving, as we did, wherever we went. Hamlet residents emerged
from their houses to wave back, or they opened their windows and
waved, and some came up to the truck to shake hands with Shō-ichi.
Several times during the day we crossed paths with the incumbent's
caravan and exchanged waves with its members. Figures waving
from across a rice plain were barely visible; even if we could not
clearly see anybody, just to be safe, we waved and bowed and shouted,
O-negai shimasu ("I entreat you"). After several hours of the ritual, I
found myself waving at any available target, including dogs, children, and, once, the life-size mannequin of a street-crossing guard.

Where groups of ten people or so converged to show their support,
calling, *Gambattei* ("Keep it up!"), or offering us cups of hot green
tea, Shō-ichi had the driver stop, and he announced that his friend
had come from America especially to endorse his candidacy. At that
point, I would climb down from the truck, take the microphone, and,
facing the group, I would deliver the one-minute greeting prepared
by Haruko. Sometimes I was applauded and people shook hands
with me. Once, I looked around after my brief speech to see where
Shō-ichi and the male drivers were, and found them only a few feet
away, their backs turned to the crowd, urinating in a ditch.

We skirted danger several times as we drove the snow-covered one-lane roads. On one occasion, Haruko at the microphone let out a horrifying shout in mid sentence: "I am Utsunomiya Shō-ichi's wife and I entreat you to elect him as—Watch out! Watch out!" An ear-splitting crash reverberated through the loudspeaker. Alarmed at how close we were to a ditch, Haruko had dropped the microphone. A few seconds of silence. Then, "I am Utsunomiya Shō-ichi's wife and I entreat you . . . ," Haruko resumed, somehow managing to ignore the six-foot drop on each side of the road into the irrigation ditches below.

We ended our tour at Unomachi, at precisely five o'clock, in time to greet the waiting crowd of townspeople. They had tied around their heads white cotton scarves on which were printed the characters for "inevitable victory," and a red sun like the Japanese flag. Shō-ichi said a few words, I gave my one-minute endorsement, and somebody presented the candidate with a bouquet of flowers.

Then, with Shō-ichi, Haruko, myself, and two of Shō-ichi's campaign chiefs in the lead, the crowd marched down the main street of the town, picking up supporters as it went. Shopkeepers who backed Shō-ichi had stayed open and emerged to the shouts and cheers of the paraders. At each open shop, we stopped, bowed, and asked for support.

Eventually about three hundred people joined us along the parade route, but it was a loosely organized rally, and though evening was closing in around us, nobody knew how much further we should walk or how to end the parade, so we occasionally drifted to a halt, only to begin again. Finally, after a few more short speeches, hastily engineered by Shō-ichi's campaign managers, the crowd dispersed and we returned to Bessho in the dark to eat dinner.

By the evening, I felt certain that Shō-ichi's cause was doomed. It was not only that the campaign seemed amateurish. Shō-ichi's camp, from my limited observation of it, consisted mainly of a motley group of relatives, old men and women manning the telephones, and friends from outside the township who could not even vote in the election. Shō-ichi had only one or two really important men among his publicly announced backers—the former middle school principal and the younger brother of the previous mayor, a well-respected man who, for political reasons, could not support Shō-ichi openly. The younger brother, as surrogate, had joined us in the open truck and occasionally Shō-ichi had taken the microphone and shouted, "I've got the younger brother of the former mayor with me!" as though that alone were sufficient reason to vote for him. Behind the scenes, Shō-ichi also drew on the aid of the many young men who had participated in the training program that sends young farmers to the United States, and, of course, the people of Bessho had rallied to his cause. Since he had only a week to campaign, however, instead of the usual two weeks, Shō-ichi's chances did not look good.

On the following day—election day—Shō-ichi was at peace with himself. Casting his vote at the primary school in town, he said his mind was at ease, because he had done as much as he could. Haruko, on the other hand, was frenetic until the end. Kneeling by the *kotatsu*, she phoned one person after another, asking for the household's votes in an intense but mechanical way, bowing over the phone as she checked off the names on her list. During the past week, Haruko had walked through Bessho and its four neighboring hamlets, visiting each of the two hundred households, to beg their members to vote for her husband.

More than Shō-ichi's political career was at stake. He had spent a good deal of money on the campaign, though nowhere near the estimated outlay of his opponent. Shō-ichi figured that he had spent almost $20,000 of his own money, and he had borrowed an equal amount from Haruko's uncle, the couple's marriage go-between. If he were elected, however, he could eventually pay his political debts out of his monthly salary of $2,000.

Seven years earlier Shō-ichi had renounced politics at Haruko's insistence. Thus his present campaign and Haruko's support of it represented a remarkable about-face for both of them. Haruko's expressed reasons for agreeing to Shō-ichi's candidacy were the same as the ones he gave: first, many of his friends and associates had urged him to run and had volunteered their aid, and second, some of the incumbent's practices had angered both of them. I suspect another reason was the support Shō-ichi had garnered from conservative quarters by serving in the Agricultural Cooperative. Running for office seven years earlier would have been a lost cause; this time the political climate had changed enough to encourage Shō-ichi to go after a long-cherished dream. Nearing his fifty-second birthday, with his agrarian reforms behind him, he knew this might be his last chance to attain significant office.

Haruko had thrown herself wholeheartedly into the campaign. In addition to knocking on doors and telephoning voters, she was in charge of welcoming and feeding the endless stream of guests who arrived at the house at all hours to pay their respects to Shō-ichi. The candidate's main role was talking to callers. Without his staff of women behind the scenes and male relatives and friends who served as chauffeurs, he could not have sat so calmly amidst the swirl around him. All the gracious hospitality, the repeated words of thanks, and the steady flow of food were coordinated by Haruko, in her brown slacks and white apron, tangled strands of straight hair falling about her face, looking not so much like the wife of a candidate for political office as an overworked, overwrought servant.

The constant ringing of the telephone and the arrivals of guests and gifts at the front door gave her not a moment to relax. Guests had to be served tea, urged to stay, and if they accepted the invitation, offered dinner. Gifts and phone calls were carefully recorded in a notebook. The most common gift, *sake*, was delivered to the entryway and hauled by Haruko into the nearest room, which happened to be the one in which I was to sleep, surrounded by crates of the national alcoholic beverage. Visitors stayed until midnight, and Haruko, who was the last person in the house to go to bed, was the first one to rise early in the morning.

All of this entertaining was facilitated by the Utsunomiyas' new house. Their old one had been demolished when the road in front of it was widened following the reorganization of the rice paddies. By taking out a mortgage to supplement the money they received from the government for the loss of their home, they were able to build a new, more comfortable one on the same land. The dark, drafty, and inconvenient house of my memories was gone, and in its place stood a handsome structure painted orange and set back off the road.

The new house was graced with many of the trappings of wealth associated with well-to-do urban families or rural landlords: pots of tall chrysanthemums stood in the entryway, which also contained a scroll painting, one of two telephones, and a doorbell that chimed. But the most significant new feature was the western-style parlor or reception room (*osetsuma*), furnished with western furniture and decor befitting a man with a broad face. This small, carpeted room contained a small love seat and two chairs covered in a floral pattern, a coffee table, a liquor cabinet, a stereo, an upright piano, a television set, and bookshelves. The wallpaper and drapes, both a subdued beige, had been chosen by Yōko, but Haruko had selected the most eye-catching item in the room: a huge Victorian chandelier. The eclectic tastes of the family and the friends who had bestowed gifts on them were further reflected in objets d'art scattered on the bookshelves and on top of the piano and television: Japanese dolls, rubber dolls, an African primitive doll with a black face and red wool hair; a clock; a replica of Rodin's *The Thinker*; and a silver sailboat in a glass case.

Different guests were entertained in different parts of the house. The western parlor was reserved for guests who had big-city or overseas ties, such as members of the overseas training program or the crew of the television station sent to interview Shō-ichi. Hamlet residents were generally received in the formal Japanese room (the one with the *tokonoma*), which resembled my old bedroom. Close family members sat around the *kotatsu* in a room off the kitchen. Unlike the old living room, the room with the *kotatsu* had windows and was level with the kitchen, and it functioned as a kind of dining room or kitchenette. These three rooms, filled with a steady stream of well-wishers, made the house feel like a Japanese inn, as Haruko and her female relatives rushed food to the separate groups of guests.

Other parts of the house afforded further evidence of the family's improved standard of living. With the exception of the western-style parlor, all the rooms roughly corresponded to rooms in the old house, but the floor plan was more convenient. A central corridor connected the entryway with the rear of the house, where the toilet and bath were located, so that it was no longer necessary to walk through bed-

Haruko in front of her new house, with her chrysanthemums arranged in the entryway.

Shō-ichi campaigning for election as head of Uwa township.

rooms to reach them. A shorter corridor off the main one led to the kitchen–dining area. Guests could enter the western room directly from the entryway or from this short corridor.

The new house was also bright, clean, and fashionably decorated. The walls in the various rooms were painted pale green, and the light wood floors in the corridors were highly polished. To be sure, the kitchen was still cluttered with unwashed dishes, and there were half-filled pots of food and electrical appliances strewn on the floor for lack of space elsewhere. The floor, however, was covered with linoleum in a Mexican-tile pattern, and although Haruko fretted about how much she disliked cleaning and tidying up, she had made some headway by assembling neatly labeled plastic containers of left-over food and condiments on the open shelves. All in all, it was the home of an "important" man, a home prepared to receive notable guests and to entertain large gatherings, functions integral to a rural political campaign where personal relationships count for so much.

On the evening of election day, while Haruko and Shō-ichi awaited the voting results at home, about a hundred of us, Bessho residents and friends of Shō-ichi's from outside the hamlet, gathered in the social hall down the road to hear the ballot count relayed by telephone from campaign workers in the main headquarters in town. Thirteen thousand people were eligible to vote out of a total population of eighteen thousand, and the typical voter turnout for a local election was eighty percent, composed of an equal number of men and women voters. Shō-ichi therefore figured he needed six thousand votes to win.

The first three telephone calls from campaign headquarters reported that Shō-ichi and the incumbent were neck and neck. The fourth telephone call, greeted with applause, reported that Shō-ichi had an edge of one hundred votes. Excitement mounted. The next call put the lead at seven hundred votes, and the crowd cheered as one of the men wrote the results on a blackboard. The final call informed the elated audience that the local television station had just announced Shō-ichi's victory with a lead of over nine hundred votes. Over ninety-one percent of the electorate had voted. Shō-ichi was the new head of Uwa, swept into office one day before his fifty-second birthday.

There was pandemonium in Bessho's social hall. People began thanking each other for working on the campaign, and someone whose hand I had shaken during our parade through town the day before even telephoned to thank me for helping Shō-ichi win. Women slipped away to the kitchen to bring out ceremonial rice balls, which they passed out to the happy crowd. Suddenly, above the din, we heard one of the men call for a traditional victory cheer. The room grew silent. Everyone stood.

"Banzai!" he shouted.

"Banzai!" they roared in response, raising both arms over their heads.

They did this three times and then a group of men lifted up the brother of the former mayor and tossed him in the air. Then the former middle school principal was tossed in the air, and more "Banzai" cheers filled the room. Some of the women were weeping.

Haruko arrived minutes later and, standing in the front of the room, she bowed low and repeated a litany of appreciation in a rush of words that emerged from her mouth like bubbles, followed by silence and then another rush of words, as though she were holding her breath and expelling it in the form of syllables. She spoke in a strained, hollow voice that reflected either fatigue or the mechanical politeness that had carried her through the campaign. Her head bowed, she finally worked herself up to tears, which seemed the expected thing to do.

Shō-ichi arrived shortly afterward, but the excitement over his entrance was cut short when it was announced that he would not stay long because he did not feel well. It seemed that minutes earlier, when he had stopped off at the central headquarters, elated campaign workers had over-exuberantly tossed him into the air, and his head had snapped back, giving him a sharp pain in his neck. He had to wear a neck brace for the rest of the week.

The days that followed were filled with more activity for the head-elect of Uwa and his wife. The local television news station sent over cameramen, and the national public broadcasting station interviewed Shō-ichi over the telephone. The prefectural newspaper carried Shō-ichi's picture and a lengthy analysis of the election. Every day at precisely seven-thirty in the morning the telephone began ringing with calls from well-wishers, and these too had to be logged in. Visitors streamed in and out of the house all day. More gifts—almost entirely crates of sake—piled up in the entryway.

For Haruko, the campaign was not yet over. The day after the election, she paid a round of visits on every one of the households in Bessho to thank people formally for their support. Wherever she stopped, she repeated the same words of thanks, like a tape recording, smiling and bowing low, in a voice and manner utterly uncharacteristic of the spontaneous person I knew:

"Thank you, thank you for your hard work. I'm sorry to have troubled you. Once again I ask your indulgence."

As soon as she left each house, her smile would disappear and she would resume her scowl, grimly determined to fulfill her obligations. In the next few days, she visited all of the houses in the five neighboring hamlets, and at each one she performed the same ritual of thanks.

Shō-ichi was officially inaugurated into office in the middle of February, and a new phase of his life began. Eschewing one of the perquisites of office—a chauffeured car—he walks the one mile to his office in town, because he does not want to appear to be putting on airs, but also because he needs the exercise: shortly after the election, he experienced chest pains diagnosed as a possible heart condition, and his doctor ordered him to lose weight and give up smoking. As part of his regimen, Haruko prepares in her electric blender a bitter herbal concoction that looks and tastes like green soil, and forces him to drink it every morning.

Once again, Haruko and Shō-ichi have little time to spend together. Shō-ichi presides over a budget of sixteen million dollars,* earmarked largely for the public school system and social welfare

*Based on the spring 1982 rate of 240 yen = U.S. $1.00.

programs—for example, for the running of a nursery and an old people's home. Like other men in public office, he finds his days and evenings are filled with numerous ceremonial obligations—giving greetings to public groups that are funded by the township, or attending the weddings and funerals of persons whose families are locally prominent or who contributed to his campaign. He and Haruko eat dinner together only about once every ten days.

Yet Haruko no longer complains that her husband is neglecting the family. When I visited her and Shō-ichi again in April, she was buoyant and looked positively youthful. The hours she had spent walking from door to door on behalf of Shō-ichi's candidacy had strengthened her legs, she said, confirming my impression that she no longer walked bowlegged. Although she was approaching her fiftieth birthday, her hair was still black: it is a family trait, and neither her elder sister nor her mother had gray hair.

Like Shō-ichi, Haruko is careful not to "put on airs." "One shouldn't suddenly start wearing fancy clothes just because one's husband has become head of the township," she explained. Nevertheless, she did feel that the wife of the township head should "pay more attention to her appearance," and she said that she had recently gone to the beauty parlor for a permanent. Wherever she goes, Haruko is careful to bow and give formal greetings; it is expected of her. As we walked along the road in conversation, she would stop talking, spin around, and bow to passing cars. She is also expected to participate in the campaigns of her husband's political backers, and in April she was back in the social hall cooking with other Bessho women, this time lending moral support to a candidate for the town assembly.

Relations between Haruko and Shō-ichi are now on an even keel, and when I visited the family in April, a glowing Shō-ichi reported that he was completely content, because he was doing what he always wanted to do, with Haruko fully behind him, in total accord with his ambitions. Obāsan too expressed a sense of tranquility, due in large part to Haruko's management of family affairs. "I no longer have any worries," she said. "My daughter-in-law is kind to me."

Bent over in her old age, her frail back not able to hold erect even her fragile body, Obāsan, seventy-three years old, had grown thinner and her coughing fits continued to disturb her mealtimes. Despite her physical deterioration, however, her state of mind was more serene than in the days when I had lived with the family. She now eats alone in her own house, because her feet hurt and she prefers not to walk to the main house for her meals. Haruko brings food to her, and she has her own small electric rice cooker. The two houses are connected by an intercom system, and several times a day Haruko spoke into it to tell her mother-in-law that she was leaving the house or to inquire whether Obāsan needed anything. Evidence of the women's increased communication was the campaign gossip Obāsan related, which Haruko had readily shared with her.

Obāsan repeated several times that she had no worries, and she also reiterated her praise for Haruko as a farm and campaign worker. "She's broken her bones" with work, the old woman said—perhaps the greatest compliment a Japanese mother-in-law can give her daughter-in-law.

The Utsunomiyas' twenty-two-year-old daughter still lives at home but teaches the second grade of primary school. After graduating from high school, Yōko attended a teachers' education college in Kyoto and passed a strict teacher certification examination with high grades. As part of her training she had to learn to play the piano, and the piano that now stands in the family's western room is hers. Dressed in a tailored skirt and jacket, Yōko commutes to work during the week in the car she bought with her earnings—$450 a month and an annual bonus equivalent to half a year's salary—and over the weekends she attends school-related conferences or takes short trips with girlfriends. She is not expected to cook.

Haruko, now the sole farmer in the family, received her driver's license six years ago and drives both the car and the pickup truck. She has also learned to operate a plow-like machine called a *kanriki*. "I'm the only woman around who can use it," she said, "and when I push it along the fields, men stare at me in surprise."

Because the tobacco crop takes up most of Haruko's work time, she no longer seeks outside employment. It is more difficult for her to grow tobacco than rice, because she is not yet completely familiar with the many stages of processing the tobacco leaf. In late November and December the tobacco is planted in small pots, and tended in greenhouses until late March and early April, when it is transplanted to unused paddy fields. The soil must be fertilized and the suckers removed to encourage growth in the leaves. The harvest is actually a continuous process of picking the leaves when they mature between the months of June and August—a period that overlaps with the transplanting season for rice and imposes a double duty on Haruko, who still helps prepare the rice paddies, along with other families in the machine cooperative. Once picked, the tobacco leaves are further processed in a series of time-consuming stages: it is necessary to rank each leaf according to its size and color on a scale of one to five, to dry the leaves in a communal operation that begins at the end of August, and finally to put them in thirty-pound bags, which are sealed mechanically. The tobacco Haruko grows on about one-half acre of land is sold through a government monopoly and yields an annual profit of about three thousand dollars.

In addition to growing tobacco and helping with the rice crop, Haruko continues to grow vegetables for the family's table, but overall the Utsunomiyas have considerably reduced their farming operations in recent years. Although they do still own a share of the mountain pig business, they have sold the ninety pigs they once raised behind their house, and after Shō-ichi's election, they reduced by one-fourth the amount of tobacco under cultivation and hired a few laborers to help Haruko with it. They rent out half of their four acres of land to another family in Bessho for about twenty-three hundred dollars a year.*

Renting farm land to others is typical of a general trend in the area. In fact, one of the main effects of the agricultural reforms implemented seven years earlier has been to reduce the number of farming households in Bessho. In 1974, thirty-nine households farmed; by

---

*The family's income, comprising Shō-ichi's salary of $24,000, $3,000 from the tobacco crop, $2,300 from the rented land, and perhaps $1,000 from rice farming and the share in the pig business, therefore amounted to about $30,000, nearly three times their income of seven years earlier. It also represented an increase of perhaps $4,000 over their income of the preceding year, when Shō-ichi earned about $14,000 from farming (mainly from the tobacco crop) and another $12,000 from the pig business; but most of this increase would go toward paying off Shō-ichi's political debts.

1982, the number had dropped to twenty-nine. In this sense, Shō-ichi's plan to rescue farming has not succeeded. Farm families who owned less than one and one-half paddy acres have discovered that it does not pay to cultivate them; it is more lucrative to rent all of their rice land to other farmers and take full-time jobs instead.* It is also more practical: as one woman said, "the reforms have made individual paddies bigger, so you can't just farm a little in one paddy, then do something else, then farm again in another paddy." At the same time, as a result of the rearrangement of the paddies and the introduction of new machinery, farmers with larger holdings can rent even more land to farm, because they now have the machinery to cultivate bigger tracts. To this extent, the agricultural reforms were a success, because it is more cost-efficient to farm on a larger scale.

There was certainly evidence of increased prosperity in Bessho. Thriving on their incomes as landlords and salaried workers, many residents had, like the Utsunomiyas, rebuilt their homes on a grander scale. There were more two-story residences than I remembered, some with large windows and roofs painted bright orange, red, or green. Splashes of colorful flowers appeared in the area in front of the houses that used to be planted with vegetables. One of the younger wives was driving a new Toyota sedan, and other women, who seven years earlier might have ridden bicycles, now drove pickup trucks. A number of residents had built garages for their vehicles. Whereas the rural population in Japan as a whole continued to decline, the population of Bessho had increased by four or five families, who worked in or near major cities in the prefecture and found it convenient to commute from the Unomachi area, where land is still available. To accommodate the heavier traffic, a two-lane road has been built through the hamlet; it is three times the width of the original, one-lane road and has a paved pedestrian walk on one side.

For all their new-found prosperity, however, Bessho families still expressed a sense of uneasiness about their futures, and when asked how they viewed the current economic situation, they invariably used the term *fukeiki*, "hard times." Paradoxically, they have survived as

*The average holding in the area is one and three-quarter acres of rice land.

farmers by not farming. They are aware that the security of their jobs as construction workers, carpenters, and the like depends on larger economic forces that have created these jobs for them, and they would feel more confident if they could derive their livelihood from the soil, doing the work they know best. Agricultural reforms, enacted to rescue farming in Japan, have removed farmers from their farms; to save their land, they have to leave it to work elsewhere.

Government policy has served further to separate farmers from farming. Because the Japanese market is oversupplied with rice, for several years the government has held down producer prices and in the Uwa area alone has removed from rice production almost one thousand acres—nearly one-fourth of Uwa's rice land. Thus, in a region with a tradition of rice farming reaching back two thousand years, a region famous for rice and for farmers experienced in producing good rice, families such as the Utsunomiyas receive a subsidy to keep their land fallow and are encouraged to grow other crops instead.

The number of Japanese households supporting themselves by farming alone has steadily declined in recent years to about ten percent. Among the few full-time farming households in Bessho is the Uesugi family. In addition to cultivating rice, tobacco, and grapes, they have invested in a vinyl greenhouse, where the younger Mrs. Uesugi now spends most of her days with her husband and mother-in-law growing strawberries for market. The trend in Japanese agriculture, however, is away from such full-time farming. Most of Japan's farmers practice farming only as a sideline to supplement their incomes. The average farm family income in 1978 was approximately seventeen thousand dollars, and only one-fourth of that amount came from farming.*

Citrus growers in the prefecture, many with holdings of only two and one-half acres, have managed to survive as full-time farmers by introducing new varieties of citrus along with the *mikan* and by building greenhouses, in which fruit may be grown all year round. By watching market conditions, they have become adept at switching

*These figures are from *Nippon: A Charted Survey of Japan* (Tokyo, 1980).

from one kind of citrus fruit to another and at developing new products derived from them, such as brandy or canned fruit, in response to changes in supply and demand.

In the fishing villages along the coast, where few factory and construction jobs are available, farmers blessed with natural resources and entrepreneurial talent have developed local industries such as pearl cultivation or fish hatcheries. In recent years the damage done to marine life by pollution in the Inland Sea has increased the commercial importance of the Uwa Sea, and Uwa's fishing villages have benefitted from the new demand for their produce. Their economic activities nevertheless remain labor-intensive and minuscule when compared with the scale of fishing operations in the United States; vulnerable to sudden changes in national and international economic conditions, the local fishing industry depends on the flexibility of its work force—frequently consisting of part-time female laborers—and on government protection for its economic survival.

If the salaried men in the countryside express anxiety about their economic security, what frightens many of the farmers is the spectre of trade liberalization, which threatens to bring in lower-priced farm products from exporting countries like the United States, Australia, and Brazil to compete with Japanese products. Between 1981 and 1982, the American government, alarmed by the unfavorable balance of trade with Japan, put pressure on the Japanese to increase imports. Among other things, it demanded that the Japanese lift their quotas on the import of farm products, and beef and citrus in particular, a demand that has met with widespread opposition in the farming communities. Many, including Shō-ichi, fear that Japanese farmers, whose operations are carried out on a much smaller scale and are less mechanized, cannot compete with their American counterparts. Even after shipping costs, the Americans can sell their agricultural produce in Japan more cheaply than Japanese farmers can. It is a reflection of the scale and technological efficiency of American agriculture that even rice—sown by helicopter across vast acreage in California—will outsell Japanese rice if allowed freely into Japan. As one of the largest importers of agricultural produce in the world, Japan already imports much of its feed grains and almost all of its wheat and soybeans from the United States.* To import even more, farmers argue, would make Japan dangerously dependent on foreign trade for its food supply. Farmers are afraid that if the government does not continue to protect farming, Japanese agriculture will disappear.

The countryside thus presents a contradictory picture of new wealth accompanied by persistent anxiety over economic conditions. In these circumstances, it is not surprising to find more farm women than ever before seeking jobs wherever they can. In Bessho, according to Haruko's estimate, every household still has at least one wage-earning woman. The hamlet's small textile factory, closed in 1974, was reopened two years later by a couple living in Bessho who owned a larger factory in another city. Six women sit in the one-room wooden building sewing different parts of men's polo shirts on sewing machines. A man operates a machine that stitches monograms on the pockets of men's golf shirts. Depending on their skill, the women earn about twelve dollars a day, working an eight-to-five day about two hundred days of the year.

In addition to working in textile factories, women are still in demand as *dokata* (construction workers), and their daily salaries have more than doubled since 1975 to about sixteen dollars. Other women work in *mikan*-canning plants, pick tea leaves, or do piecework at home on sewing machines—for example, sewing buttons on blouses. One of Haruko's neighbors, who once worked with her on a ditch-digging team, recently passed a course that certified her to work as a cook: she prepares meals at the newly opened restaurant of nearby Akeishi temple.

In the numerous small industries along the coast, women are still relied upon to perform a wide variety of tasks. For example, a group of women in one village kneel on the ground and separate tiny sardines, arranging them by size, while other women stand indoors at large, steaming cauldrons washing the catch, and still others dry the fish on the ground in the sun. The end product finds its way into sealed plastic bags of dried fish, which are sold for about sixty cents in urban food stores.

*Japan Economic Yearbook, 1981–82 (Tokyo, 1982), p. 41.

Women in another village do the delicate work of inserting into the bodies of oysters the small bead that stimulates the growth of pearls. A group of five or six women sit in a one-room wood shack a few feet from the sea, where the oyster beds bob under water, and using tools that look as if they might have come from a dentist's office, they perform the sensitive operation that, if done properly, results in the production of a gleaming pearl; if done improperly, it kills the oyster.

Farm women thus remain vital to the continuity of agriculture in Japan, serving as a flexible, comparatively inexpensive work force. If there is any outward change in their work lives, it is in the clothing they wear: although women workers still favor bonnets, white scarves around their necks, and aprons, they have discarded both traditional pantaloons and jeans in favor of the work clothes popular among male farmers—jogging pants with white stripes down the side of the pant legs.

"What are your future goals and aspirations?" Haruko suddenly asked me on the night before my departure from Bessho. Surprised to learn that I did not have any in particular, she gave me a pitying look. Haruko was very clear about her own future. "There are three more subjects that belong in your book," she said: "my daughter's wedding, my relations with my son's wife, whoever she will be, and my duty of nursing my mother-in-law in her final days."

Shō-ichi too has set specific goals for himself. He hopes to run for re-election for two more terms, a total of twelve years, and then retire from public office. By that time Hisashi, who is now a freshman in the horticultural college outside of Tokyo that Shō-ichi attended, will have graduated and returned to live with them. Although Hisashi has expressed willingness to inherit the farm and even helps Haruko with the tobacco crop during his summer vacation, in all likelihood he will have to get a job locally, perhaps as a high school teacher, because, like most Japanese farmers, he will not be able to support his family on farming alone.

Although I could not stay to see the fulfillment of the Utsuno-miyas' life plans, I no longer had any doubts about their prospects of success. It was obvious that they were riding on top of the changes that were transforming the old rural society of their youth.

When I left Shō-ichi for the final time on the platform of the Uno-machi train station where we had first met seven years earlier, he was wearing his brown business suit and looked like the salaried man of every farm woman's dreams. Haruko, meanwhile, who was going with me as far as Matsuyama for a shopping spree with a friend, had on a navy blue skirt, a blouse, and heels, and looked for all the world like her old description of herself, "only a housewife." Both husband and wife had almost fully emerged from the farm class, shedding their former social identities like skins.

Gone were the pig farmers of only seven years earlier. Gone too was their drafty house with its kitchen full of flies from the pigsty. And the old rice paddies with their jigsaw-puzzle shapes had all but vanished. Once they had been worked by small groups of men and women nearly hidden by the tall rice stalks; the new, rectangular paddy fields yielded to combines and tractors and mechanical rice-transplanters. The old patterns of land and labor were disappearing, and in their place were the new preoccupations of commuting workers and consumers, people who answered doorbells that chimed, stored leftover food in Tupperware plastic containers, and sat on couches to serve their American guests whiskey, wine, and brandy, in that order, as aperitifs before dinner.

The deeper things had survived: Shō-ichi's quiet assurance, Haruko's warmth and whimsicality, and her wholly traditional "future goals and aspirations." But at the Utsunomiya house and wherever else in Bessho the eye fell, the message was clear: a way of life a millennium old would soon be gone beyond recall.